Nurturing Grandchildren
Black, White & In-between

Written & Illustrated by Jean Moule, PhD

Cover: Jean's Grandchildren in Alaska; photo chosen by Bella, 10.
Back Cover: Some Skipping Stones Issues with Jean's Columns.
This Page: Jean and four of her Grandchildren in 2005 & 2007.

Edited by Arun N. Toké
Published by Skipping Stones, Inc.

Nurturing Grandchildren

Welcome to *Nurturing Grandchildren: Black, White & In-between.* This book may be a resource for all grandparents and of special interest for grandparents of multicultural children. Perhaps you were not excited when your child decided to choose a partner across racial lines. Like my parents, and others, you may have said, "What about the children?" Yet when you first held that beige baby some of your fears melted and your heart became filled with care for that child.

As a mother of biracial children and a grandmother to multi-racial children, and as professor whose most popular class is "Racial and Cultural Harmony," I have ideas and experiences on how to help love and raise children whose very existence is a bright hope for our nation still beset by racial strife.

President Barack Obama, a child of a White mother and a Black father, received unconditional love from his White grandparents. This love was essential for his strength and achievements. Each of us have opportunities to influence our world and those around us. Grandparents of biracial children have a unique role and few resources.

My hope is that these one-page columns over a nine-year-period from *Skipping Stones: Multicultural Literary Magazine,* will help strengthen and give resources to parents and grandparents of brown and other color children. Each section of the book begins with my watercolor art, a letter from an individual who knows our family, continues with columns from the magazine, and ends with excerpts from my academic work on biracial children and families.

Jean Moule, PhD

© 2015 by Nana Jean & Skipping Stones, Inc. All Rights Reserved.

Table of Contents

- 3 **Family**
  - 5 Reflections on Childhood
  - 6 On Love
  - 7 Family Connections
  - 8 Cookies and a Circle of Care
  - 9 **Understanding Bicultural Families**
- 11 **Skin Deep**
  - 12 About Skin Color
  - 13 Are You White? Are You Black?
  - 14 About Hair
  - 15 About Swimming
  - 16 About Biracial Identity
  - 17 On Racial Identity in Children
  - 18 Blink of the Eye Racism
  - 19 **Understanding Bicultural Children**
- 21 **Encouraging Passionate Pursuits**
  - 24 Using Your Gifts to Make New Friends
  - 25 Expanding Horizons
  - 26 Cousins' Country Camp
  - 27 Learning by Working Together
  - 28 On Geocaching
  - 29 Cultivating Focused Human Beings
  - 30 On Creativity
  - 31 **Nurturing Grandchildren**
- 35 **Global Customs and Cultures**
  - 36 On Deep Culture
  - 37 On New Perspectives
  - 38 Aloha from the Birthplace of a Biracial President
  - 39 Hawai'i: Cultures and Families in the 50th State
  - 40 Cycle of Enlightenment
  - 41 Cultural Connections
  - 42 What I Learned about Grandparenting in China
  - 43 On European Customs
  - 44 What's in a Name?
  - 45 **Understanding Cultures**
- 47 **Inspiring Role Models**
  - 48 Bessie Coleman: African American Aviatrix
  - 49 Jean Faces A Challenge
  - 50 Rosa Parks: One Person Can Make A Difference
  - 51 On Speaking Up
  - 52 About Role Models Like Yourself
  - 53 Let's Make a Difference in Our World
  - 54 **Continuing On**

Reflections on Origins, Love, and Times Together

Family

She shall be like a tree planted by the rivers of water... (Psalm 1)

This 400 year old oak stands visible from our house and borders our garden.

From my own beginnings, to the love of my life, to stories of our children and grandchildren, this oak symbolizes where we are planted and how our lives have changed and grown over the years.

A Letter from My Forever Friend and Neighbor

Jean,

I am undone by how honored I am, to be asked to write down my feelings and words for "family" that I have from connections with the Moule family! Thanks for always being there, even when I was growing. I and my family are the richer, to call you our friends, our family. Thank you.

Each time with your grandkids is epic for me! Thanks for sharing them. When you said they could come visit, I sent a quick text to Stu/Opa, "Jamie and Chance have asked to come up, hurry home!" I told our forever neighbor/friend Jean to send them up in an hour, as Stu was in town, but now I regret that they aren't here yet. I shared with Jean that I wanted time with her grandkids, squelching her thoughts that I am too full of my own grandchildren that I love to spend time with, as I have nine, all boys 1-9 years of age.

There is always time for more grandchildren, as we claim Moules' grandkids too. The time here with us is never enough though. We hold the new chickens, play in the hammocks, pick raspberries, swing on ropes, play Whack-a-Mole, bumper pool, foosball, ping-pong, tetherball, and squeeze in a game of Quirkle before their Cousin's Camp Program Preview and before going back to Nana and Pops' house.

I hadn't always been color sensitive. I am embarrassed to say that in college I washed my hands after a dance class where I held the hand of a non-white person. I even told Jean and Rob, from the backseat of their car this story. When describing the snowman our four young girls had made in rural Oregon while visiting my color-prejudiced parents, I said, "We used carrots for the nose, rocks for the mouth and [the slang word for Brazil Nuts] for the eyes." The "word" literally slid out of my mouth, not knowing the correct term, but with instant regret!

My ignorance and wrong teaching was replaced with wisdom on the color of your skin. The Moule family, I regard, as not only forever friends/neighbors, but as family. When our four daughters were young, we thought about who we'd want to rear them if we were to die, and we asked them to be the ones. We experienced community or family with the Moules as we dwelt together a few years, shared vacations, and hosted a home fellowship that included worship, games, and weekly potlucks.

The richness of our time spent with the Moule family is reflected in our children's request of all color of dolls, especially Black dolls!

Oodles of love,

Patty/Oma

Photo: A reptile Cousins Camp activity with daughter Mary (with snake), Grandkids, Patty and Stu (Oma and Opa)

Nana Jean Reflects on Childhood

My grandchildren are beginning to tell stories and sing new songs. Their artwork often illustrates their favorite places. As they begin to use more words, I am planning to help them construct poems of their childhood. Perhaps you would like to write a poem, too.

Under each of the topics below, you list as many words as you like. Then you add some colorful adjectives or descriptions.

• Items found around your house • Items found in your yard • Items found in your neighborhood • Names of relatives, especially those that link you to your past • Sayings your family used/uses • Names of foods • Names of places you keep your childhood memories •

Using these examples I wrote the following during a group activity:

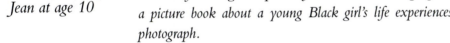

Jean at age 10

I am from the untouched, unused living room,

the stone terraza floors and too much TV.

I am from the manicured lawns fertilized by our Mexican-American gardeners

and the fig tree so big I could hide in the leaves high above the ground.

I am from a quiet city neighborhood, the playground

across the street and the one block I could roller skate around and around and around.

I am from the overworked, single mother, and the distant father.

I am from plenty of everything except family.

I am from a mother who could pass for White and a father who always wore a hat so that he wouldn't darken.

And, I am from a child who loved to spend time in nature and read the following book...and understood the experience.

*The following excerpts are from **I Wonder Why** by Shirley C. Burden (Doubleday, 1963), a picture book about a young Black girl's life experiences. Each statement is illustrated by a photograph.*

"I wonder why some people don't like me.

I like rain…and cool woods…

I like clouds floating in a blue sky…and birds…and cats…and little puppies.

I like the sea when it wears diamonds…and sand when it

squeezes through my toes…

I like flowers in spring…and lambs…and babies…

I wonder why some people don't like me."

This last line of the book is under a photo of a young Black child.

Poems and stories like this help us understand why and how we experience the world around us. A special book we have enjoyed reading to our multiracial family is **The Hello, Goodbye Window** by Norton Juster *(Hyperion, 2005)*. In this book the Black grandmother is named Nanna and the White grandfather is named Poppy. It is good for my grandchildren to see a book that has grandparents that look like their Nana and Pops!

Bella & Quinci. Photo by Angela Freeman

On Love

"The difference between an obstacle and a stepping stone is how high you lift your feet."

Love has many forms. In relationships, "unconditional love" allows each person to enjoy and appreciate others based on their very being, not their behavior. Teachers call this giving students "permanent value."

How has love held our family together? While faith is part of this bond, the love among members of our family has been expressed in unique ways. In 1964, my husband wrote:

"If I could live on grassy slopes,
And see the world through pines,
I'd culminate my fondest hopes,
And build a home yours and mine."

While we have built a physical presence, our efforts for a "family together means home," are more important.

When President Kennedy was shot in 1963, we were both attending the University of California at Berkeley. As the news swept the campus, many students found their way to the student union to listen to the broadcasts. In the midst of floor-to-floor solemn people, one man rested his head on a woman's torso. An art student at the time, I thought them an interesting picture and began to draw to pass the time and take my mind off the tragedy.

Some people may say of their beloved, "I loved you before I knew you." I can say to Rob, "I drew you before I knew you." Within days, through a dorm mate—the woman in the drawing—I met Rob (who soon became *my* Robbie).

I was smitten by Rob's poetry, which sometimes came daily. We hiked and enjoyed motorcycle rides around the Bay. After a few months I accepted his proposal that we be married the following June.

When we think of our early romantic days, one scene stands out. We were newlyweds, traveling to Salt Lake City to meet my father and his wife, before continuing by car to the East Coast for the rest of our honeymoon.

On the bus trip, we noticed a woman walking the aisles and talking to the other passengers. As she came even with us, we heard her say, "…and they even have the nerve to be wearing rings." We found out later that there was still a law on the books in Utah against interracial marriages.

We decided it was safest to wait in a dark movie theater until it was time to meet my parents. When we went to the hotel, we were told there was no record of a room reserved for us by my father. We then asked for my parents, who should have arrived. The clerk could not find their name on the register either.

We slowly walked out of the hotel with little money and no idea of how to contact my father in this hostile environment. On our way out, we glanced into the hotel dining room and saw my parents, eating and waiting for us.

My father went to the desk and insisted that we be given a room. He and his wife had had no problem registering because they were both Black. During our courtship and our marriage, this is the most blatant discrimination we have faced.

As a couple we like to travel, ski and spend time with our grandchildren. We're not sure, but we think part of the glue for our love is our determination to answer the naysayers to our marriage who inevitably said, "This marriage may work for you, but what about the children?"

When they were teenagers, one of our sons said, "If I tried to draw a picture of how much the two of you love each other, it would take a lot more hearts than what is shown on this card…I am very grateful to both of you for being together and for a solid family."

Our other son added, "…What is most important for me now is knowing wherever I am I can always come home or call home and find two loving and supporting parents. That number, two, is so important to me; people have told me they almost can't believe what a relationship the two of you have, and I realize how fortunate I really am."

These sons are in their 30s now, with children of their own. In December 2010, during a family visit, we were all around the dinner table when a blood clot entered Robbie's brain, causing a stroke that did not allow him to talk coherently. We had him at the hospital emergency room within eight minutes. Thankfully, he was given medication that relieved the blood clot, restoring his ability to talk.

Before Robbie was given the medication, he was asked to give his name, age, and tell where he was. He could not do it. Then the doctor pointed to each of our sons and asked him to speak their names. He could not do it. Finally, the doctor pointed to me, his wife of 45 years. Robbie looked into my eyes, and I could see him trying to get some words out. He could not say my name. A couple of words did come through: "my love." The emergency room crew collectively exhaled, and one son started crying.

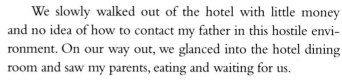

This poem came from Robbie on a Valentine's Day: *"The Love we've shared since sixty-three*
Has grown beyond just you and me.
Our three beige babes have left the nest
And the years ahead may be the best."

Family Connections

In July 2013, my husband of 48 years, Robbie, celebrated his 70th birthday. We live in Oregon, as do his two brothers and our son. Our other son lives in San Francisco, and our daughter lives in New York. To mark this special milestone in Robbie's life, I invited some who knew him to an event at our home. Both sons and his brothers surprised Robbie that late sunny afternoon. We exchanged stories and took photos.

I had a brilliant idea: Why not go around the long table and ask each person how many years they had known Robbie and the nature of their relationships? There were both light comments, for example, from a couple who had only known him a week, as well as deeper connections from people who had known him for over 40 years.

At one point, Angela, my daughter-in-law, spoke. She said that when her father died a couple of years ago, Robbie told her that from then on he would be her father. Angela had two children before she married my son. We have tried to include Quinci and Jaylin in many of our close family times, though they are older than the rest of our grandchildren, who are often pictured with me in my columns. Jaylin, at age 20 and in the middle of his undergraduate years in college, wrote a birthday note that brought tears down my cheeks:

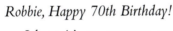

Robbie, Happy 70th Birthday!

I hope it's an awesome one, and that this decade is full of love, adventure, and blessings. And who knows, you might even get some great-grandkids. You should know that I truly admire you, and hope to be as responsible, caring, and easygoing as you are when I grow up. I'm quite thankful to have you in my life.

Love,   Jaylin

Family and love extend beyond those with biological connections. Thank you, Jaylin, for making it very clear.

With families spread across the country it is a challenge to spend time together. One way of connecting with our spread apart grandchildren is a yearly gathering of cousins. Our eighth year of the Cousin's Camp for the four grandchildren also brought their parents and other friends to our home for their annual program. This year's theme was "Plants." The kids dressed as a blackberry, a tree, a flower and a sword fern (with a plastic sword). We gathered to watch the children play in their costumes and sing the lyrics to "Invasive Species in the House Tonight," "Planting Awesome," and "Popsie's Plants are Growing."

After the event, while the kids hugged the huge oak in our front yard, the strong women that hold our family together had a moment of closeness *(see photos)*.

Family trees include branches grafted in, and the life of love and good character results in the fruit the branches bear. As a networker and resource finder, I have been able to connect my grandchildren and others with skills within my family. While Great Grandmommy Mary Ann has the children for her grandmommy cooking school, my son taught in the teacher education program I worked with at Oregon State University. I have had the privilege of bringing my professional career and my family even closer when I co-taught an on-line class first with my daughter, a lawyer in New York City, and later with my daughter-in-law in Portland, a school principal. My other daughter-in-law, a meteorologist, can give me insights into the weather as I learn to fly. What a joy to have reasons beyond family to bring our expertise together for the good of others while enjoying each other's company!

Below: Daughter Mary; Daughter-in-laws, Jenn and Angela; Jean and her mom, Mary Ann. Photos by Stu Chalupsky.

Cookies and a Circle of Care

Grandmommy's oatmeal raisin cookies have a special place in our hearts and stomachs. She baked and brought some to every gathering, sent care packages away to school, and brought basketfuls as a gift when she was a house guest. She baked other varieties and other goods, but the oatmeal raisin cookies are what everyone loves.

How did she come to cook for others? Food and feeding have an emotional and physical role for caregivers. Mothers of children who are different from those around them due to skin color, or disability, or something that makes the child especially vulnerable, are often particularly protective of those children. Mothers who have themselves had difficult childhoods may, for example, feed their children often and much because they had a food scarcity while young. Grandmommy was an orphan and raised by an aunt with limited money and affection to share.

Those cookies may symbolize Grandmommy's care for our family. Such care is often returned.

In Grandmommy Mary Ann's case, she shared her love of cooking through "Grandmommy's Cooking School." Each summer for ten years, my youngest grandkids have gathered for Cousins Camp. Each year, for six years, one day of the Cousins Camp was spent in Grandmommy's kitchen in Salem, Oregon.

She made shirts that said "Grandmommy's Cooking School" and the four children wrote their names on their shirts each year. Those shirts have served as aprons and brought continuity from year to year.

In Grandmommy's home they learned to make cupcakes, pizza, macaroni and cheese, apple turnovers, chocolate goodies, and smoothies. The kitchen was filled with the smell of fresh baking or the icy feel of the berry smoothies on little tongues.

Especially for my grandchild who has no siblings, this time with his cousins is particularly meaningful. He gets to join a larger circle of family while he also participates in the cycle of life and learning from one generation to another.

As Grandmommy got older, it took more time and energy to make batches of this delicious treat. She just stopped making oatmeal raisin cookies last year when she was 88 years old. Last Thanksgiving she flew across the country to visit one set of great grandchildren with that last batch safely tucked into her carryon bag.

This month, Grandmommy left her larger home, with full kitchen and oven for baking, and moved into an independent living community.

Many family members and family friends, formerly treated with cookies, are now returning her kindness to help her move into a smaller place with large windows, friendly neighbors, but no oven.

We helped her move room-by-room to her new place. First the living room, with places to sit and family photos on the shelves. Then the tiny kitchen, with enough dishes and appliances to fix her own breakfasts.

Next came her bedroom and clothing in anticipation of her first night on the 14th floor, overlooking Portland, Oregon, her new home.

As more friends and family came to help, she moved her last treasures to Portland. How delightful to go through her photos and personal effects with her as she decided what to keep and what to pass on.

Finally, she was settled into her new home. Her enthusiasm as she meets new friends and tries new activities reminds me of the first days on a college campus or a vacation on a cruise ship.

When family members come to the residents' dining hall she describes her favorite new meals and desserts, but we know they won't be as good as her oatmeal raisin cookies. Then she introduces us to her new friends. How wonderful to see her charms come through as she greets people near the elevator or at her table in the dining room.

A circle is complete. Goodies out and kindness and support in.

—*Jean Moule, with the help of her sister Patricia and daughter Mary.*

Our Family Gathering at Christmas, 2014

Understanding Bicultural Families

There are two kinds of bicultural families, those in which the parents come from different cultures and others in which parents from the same culture have adopted a child from another culture. Bicultural families and children are on the increase. In 2010, an estimated 1.6 million interracial married couples inhabited the United States, an increase of about 900 percent since 1965 when I entered an interracial marriage. Although still a small percentage of all couples in the United States, interracial couples are becoming more common.

Recent evidence indicates that children of mixed racial heritage may be more stable than other children. Bicultural children are quite capable of developing healthy ethnic identities and finding a stable social place for themselves. Rather than having to choose membership in one group over the other, healthy identity development involves integrating both cultural backgrounds into a single sense of self that is a blend of both and yet uniquely different from either. Bicultural children welcome the opportunity to discuss and explore who they are ethnically with family members. Individuals who are uncomfortable with the idea of intercultural relationships may project their own discomfort onto the children. As a longtime member of an interracial marriage, I remember well my own family's concerns in this area as you read in the pages of this book.

A Letter from My Daughter in New York City

Dear Mom/Jean,

When you asked me to introduce this section of your new book, I thought, how could I possibly have anything to add to your vast lived experience and intellectual research into the topic of multicultural families? But then it hit me: until I was born, you didn't have any experience with biracial children. Here are some reflections from your first guinea pig.

While your children were growing up, you and Dad focused on raising children with good character, positive self-worth, and a charitable outlook on the world. Living as an interracial family in a strongly mono-racial community, we didn't talk very much about race and racial difference, unless we were addressing a stereotypical remark made by others or filling out forms for the census or standardized tests. With my beige-ish skin, blond-ish hair and blue-ish eyes, people often assumed that I am White. But when they saw me with my family, there was no question that I am Black.

It wasn't until I arrived at Williams College (an increasingly less mono-racial community), that I really began to think about what it meant for me to be a biracial individual in a world that preferred to put people into clear-cut categories. In my own quest to understand my identity, I joined the Black Student Union, did a concentration in African-American Studies, and engaged in academic research into racial identity, eventually interviewing other multiracial individuals and writing a senior thesis on the Identity Development of Mixed-Race Individuals.

Meanwhile, our family was engaging on a similar journey. My brothers each explored their own racial identity in college, you and Dad developed a more diverse group of friends, and you embarked on your own academic exploration of racial identity in college and racial difference in the classroom, acquiring knowledge which you have been able to share with your students in the College of Education at Oregon State University. We even taught a distance learning class together, in which we both brought our experiences and research to the virtual table.

Now that I have children of my own, I, too, try to help Ainsley and Jamie develop in positive and productive ways. For them, that includes helping them understand their own racial identity and the bridging function that they can play in the diverse communities in which they live, learn, and play. We talk about race and racial identity and inequality and opportunity. They benefit from and contribute to the diversity around them. And they have blossomed under the positive influence of their two Black and two White grandparents.

Whether they eventually choose to be Black, White, or biracial, they have the knowledge and experience to make their own choices. Thank you for that!

Love,

Mary

Photo: Mary with her siblings, Matt and Michael

Reflections on Color, Hair, and Identity

Skin Deep

We are each born into the world with varying physical characteristics that influence how we are seen by others and how we see ourselves. These columns, written for and about my multihued children and grandchildren, may help us all as we grow from preexisting roots and relate to those around us.

Ask Nana Jean about Skin Color

Why are people different colors?

The tone of human skin can vary from a dark brown to a nearly colorless pigmentation, which appears pale pink due to the blood in the skin. Skin color is based on the amount of melanin[1] in the skin. In general, people who live near the Equator have darker skin and people who live far from the Equator have lighter skin because they have adapted to more or less exposure from the sun.

How do children learn about different color of skin?

I have a friend who tells the story of going to the bank with her daughter who lived in an all-White community. While holding onto her mother's hand, she stretches around to get a good look at the man in front of her from both sides and then says, "Look mommy, a chocolate man." In a situation like that, rather than telling the child she'd said something bad, she calmly explained that different people have different skin colors and that all skin tones are beautiful.

Until I was about eight years old, I didn't know about races. I thought everyone was the same. Mom was a lot lighter than we were and my sister was a little darker and younger than I was, so I figured that people's skin stretched as they got older!

One of my grandchildren describes her family members like this: "brownish, whitish, tan, honey."

Why do children learn to be afraid of people who have different skin tones?

It is hard not to get the idea that certain skin tones are more valuable in our country because of the way people of different colors are shown in the movies, advertisements and on TV. Also, parents may accidentally teach their children that certain skin tones are "scary." Babies begin to learn racism when they are just months old. For example, a White mother in an elevator is holding her five-month-old baby. A Black person gets on the elevator, and the mother tightens her grip. The baby experiences "threat" or "danger."

Have you ever had someone treat you badly because of the color of your skin?

Yes, many times, even now. Racism is not as open as when I was a child. When my sister and I were children, we went to South Carolina by plane and we had a stopover in Florida. We were *so* hungry and there was a hot dog stand about twenty feet from where we were sitting and mom wouldn't get us any food. She didn't have the heart to tell us that they wouldn't have served us because, at that time, some people would discriminate[2] against people with dark skin.

Is it like this in other countries as well?

In other places in the world, color of skin is treated differently. Sometimes worse and sometimes better. My sister told me, "When I was in Holland years ago, I noticed that the Dutch seem to be colorblind. It was so strange not to be looked at as a *brown-skinnned* person first."

Sometimes people think I am from another country because my skin is not White. What could I say?

The North American continent had brown-skinned people living here long before any White people came here. Except for the Native Americans, most of our ancestors were from other continents. So this person does not know history very well. I might answer this question this way: "I am from the United States of America with some ancestry from the continent of Africa. I have not learned the specific country,…yet."

My teacher sometimes mixes me up with my friend who is also Asian. What should I say?

Sometimes, when people look at people who are very different in skin tone from their own family and friends, they have a harder time telling people apart. When this happens to me, I usually just smile and tell them that I am not that person. It is very frustrating, but I think that kindness is the best response. You might say: "Oh, that was not me, I think I know who you meant though." Or "You must have mistaken me for someone else."

Why are your grandchildren all different colors?

Because my husband is White, some people would say that our children were going to be so "beautiful because mixed kids look cuter." It is better to use the term "multiracial." I think our children and our grandchildren are a beautiful range of color, I think all skin tones have beauty in them. How fortunate you are if you live in a place where you can see people of all different colors.

[1] *Melanin is a colored pigment that is found in skin and hair. Melanin protects from sunburn.*

[2] *Discrimination based on skin color is called racism.*

Are You White? Are You Black?

Are you White? Are you Black? Biracial children may hear this question. How do they respond?

Imagine a mother holding her newborn in her arms and noticing that the baby's skin color is different from her own. What is she thinking? How does she feel? My daughter-in-law said her first thought was, "Whose baby is that?" when her child with lighter skin-tone was born. When my first child was born, my roommates in the hospital room said, "Are you sure that is your baby?"

Now that baby can be identified in all her racial categories on the United States Census Form. It was not always this way.

My biracial daughter, my first child, was born in 1969. As an African American, I was surprised when the doctor who examined her when she was 7 weeks old listed her as "White female." Mary has been listed in 5 census reports now. In 1970, regardless of what the doctor said, I checked "Black" for her. In 1980, I asked her how she would like to be listed. At age 10, it was a difficult and emotional moment for her. Should she put "Black" like her mother? Or "White" like her father?

I must admit that after Mary was born I prayed, "Dear God, next time, I would like a little boy, with brown hair, and brown eyes, and brown skin." I know now that it makes Mary sad. I loved her very much with her wavy blond hair and blue eyes. At the time, though, I was the only person with brown skin in my church, my neighborhood, my town! In fact, according to the 1970 census, there were only 22 African Americans out of 72,000 people in my county! I wanted to hold a child that was brown like me.

In the 1980 census, Michael, the answer to that prayer, decided to check the "Black" Box. Mary checked off "White."

In the 1990 census, Mary identified herself as "Black."

Finally, in 2000, Mary had the option, if she chose it, of checking two different races on the census form.

In the 2010 Census, Mary (see left) and her husband, both biracial, checked just one box: "Black." And that's what they chose for their two children.

How do biracial and multi-racial children feel about having parents of different skin tone?

Mary's first child, a girl, is of noticeably darker color than her parents and her younger brother. What does she think? She says her family is "brownish, whitish, tan, honey."

Regardless of parents' viewpoints on racial identity there are various, thoughtful reasons for thinking about race and racial identity in different ways in different families. For some people, there may be a need to identify a certain way because of the surrounding community. Family conversations about racial identity may or may not help with understanding your place in the community or the world. More important is gaining broad horizons and the self-confidence that allow children to figure these (and many other) things out for themselves. That may be much more important than an early exposure to multicultural identity.

And while race still matters in both small and large ways, it is my hope that someday Martin Luther King Jr.'s words will become true: "I have a dream that my four little children will one day live in a nation where they will not be judged by the color of their skin but by the content of their character."

It is easier than ever to appreciate the richness of having parents of two or more racial backgrounds now that our President is biracial. My hope is that

"beige babies" will be increasingly appreciated and valued as part of our multi-ethnic, multi-cultural nation. The book, *Shades of Black: A Celebration of Our Children* (*Scholastic*) gives us a glimpse of these multi-hues called Black: *I am…creamy white…and silky smooth brown/ And…golden brown/ I am…velvety orange…and…coppery brown/ I am…radiant brassy yellow…and…gingery brown/I am Black. I am unique.*

Ask Nana Jean about Hair

My name is Jean Golson Moule. I was born in South Carolina. I moved to New York City with my parents and went to school in the Bronx when it was primarily Jewish. I was the only African American child in my classroom.

Ainsley, 12

When we moved to Los Angeles, California, I went to very multiethnic/multiracial schools from second grade through high school. I have three children and six grandchildren. They all call me Nana. On the previous page you see my four youngest grandchildren and my latest hairstyle.

Many African-American women with long, dark, curly/braided hair get questions or comments like these: *How do you get your hair like that?, How do you get your hair to do that cool twisty thing?, Can I try braiding it, or twisting it?, or, Can I touch your hair?*

Often, we tell them, "Sure! Can I touch yours?"

A fourth grade teacher told me, "My hair is huge; it's kinky, messy and untamed. It's very wild stuff. As a teacher, I am used to kids asking to touch it. Some adults I am meeting for the first time also ask to touch my hair. I generally don't mind. After having an entire class of fourth graders run their hands through my hair, anything else goes! With people I don't know very well, it isn't comfortable, but I say *'Yes,'* However, for many people this would be awkward at best, and offensive at worse. So say, *'I like your hair, may I touch it?'* Be polite, don't assume, think, 'Would you like someone touching your hair, even when they ask you nicely?'"

My hair grows this way. I wear it natural (I now wear it in locks). Sometimes, other Black people compliment me and inquire about where my locktician is located. Years ago, when I used to wear braids or twists, I'd get a few comments now and again from non-Black people. *Would you share your beauty secrets?*

I wash my hair with water and shampoo, like most people. But since I have locks, some kids and even adults assume I don't wash my hair. When White people want to grow locks, they have to let the oils build up in the hair so that it will lock. People with thinner hair can't wash theirs often or the locks will come out.

If someone asks me, *"How do you cut your hair?,"* I am tempted to say, "Scissors are good. How do you cut yours?" But I might simply answer: "At the barber shop or the beauty salon."

Some curious girls ask me: *How long does it take to do your hair? or, Do you braid your hair everyday?*

The initial braiding of the hair depends upon many variables, like the style of the braids, the skill of the braider and the thickness of the hair of the person receiving the service. Time investment ranges from two to ten hours for the braider to complete the task. Also, braids generally require daily maintenance.

If you ask questions like: *Why do you flatten your hair out sometimes?, Does that mean you don't think it's beautiful when it's curly and energetic and woolly?, or, Why do you change your hair so often?* I may say, "Because I like change. Because I can. Because it's fun."

Some African American women straighten their hair for the look, manageability, pressure to conform or personal preferences. Others choose natural styles.

If you are seriously interested in African American hair, I recommend: **Hair Story: Untangling the Roots of Black Hair in America** *(Byrd & Tharps, 2001).* The book covers topics ranging from the management of Black hair in Africa during the 1400s, to the lack of choice of hair management during the times of slavery, to the choices of hair management in modern times.

Glossary

Locked hair: Also called dreadlocks, locks or dreads. They are matted ropes of hair which will form by themselves if the hair is allowed to grow naturally without the use of brushes, combs, razors or scissors for a long period of time. Although the term dread lock was originally associated with the Rastafarian community, people of various cultures wear locks.

Locktician: Someone who specializes in the care of hair that is locked, may include initial locking, maintenance, and styling.

Bella, 10

Chance, 10

Summer's Coming! Ask Nana Jean about Swimming

Summer is coming and with it, opportunities to swim and play in the water. Nana Jean hopes you are safe near water, and that you will learn to swim if you have not learned already.

Amazingly, some people, because of their experiences, have questions about African Americans and swimming.

I have never seen an African-American in my neighborhood pool or on the Olympic Swimming Team. Can Black people swim?

If you live somewhere that is highly segregated you may not have seen someone of African descent swim, so I understand that you may wonder if Black people can swim! Read the questions and answers below to help you understand why some Blacks do and some don't.

Isn't swimming like most things? That is, race has little to do with ability?

Yes, some African Americans can swim very well. Someone I knew laughed when I asked him if he could swim. He said, "Are you serious?.... Not only can I swim, I was a certified lifeguard at the age of 18 and have saved several individuals from drowning."

Does where you live make a difference on whether you learn to swim?

An African American woman told me, "In Inglewood, where I grew up, there were no pools in which to swim, no golf courses or tennis courts. Only basketball and track fields. I learned when I was 30 years old." Another Black friend told me, "I can swim; my brother was a junior lifeguard at the closest YMCA. It took us forever to walk to the pool in the summer because our poor neighborhood did not have backyard swimming pools or adequate funding for public facilities with pools. Even today, the parents of poor children do not have the disposable income necessary to pay for private swimming lessons."

What are other reasons people do not learn to swim?

My own mother, who is 83, never learned to swim. In her childhood, public pools had "Whites Only" signs.

Also, some religions require women to show less skin in public. However, there are companies that make swimsuits that cover the whole body.

Shouldn't everyone learn to swim?

I think so. Some high schools or colleges require students to learn to swim. One person told me, "Yes, I can swim, but only because it was a requirement of my undergraduate degree. All undergraduates had to enroll in and pass a swimming course."

Nana Jean, can you swim?

Swimming was a requirement in my high school and that's when I really learned to swim. The African-American girls, who usually had their hair straightened in those days, dreaded having the class first period. Just a little bit of water and we would have a bad hair day. I remember putting a thick layer of hair oil under the edge of my swimming cap in order to keep the water out and my straightened hair straight. I think some of us said we were beginning swimmers even if we were better than that just because then we would not have to put our heads under the water as much. But you had to pass the swimming test, or you had to take the class again. A lot of girls became better swimmers during the last week of class. So I would say that at the age of 15, I could sort of swim, but my hair couldn't!

Now, I wear my hair in locks and I really like to swim. I have swum across a lake, I have taken part in a triathlon (swimming, biking, and running) and I have jumped into water with ice in it and swum a very short distance. Refreshing!!

How about you, reader? Can you swim?

About Biracial Identity

What race is presidential candidate Barack Obama?

Barack Obama, the child of a Kenyan father and a White mother from Kansas, is an example of the many biracial, multiracial, multicultural, and multi-ethnic people who are born and live in the United States. As you can see from the many photos in this book, my grandchildren are of varying colors. When my husband, who is White, and I were married in 1965, he wrote me a poem about how our family would have beige babies.

Granddaughter Bella

Two of our biracial children married people who are also biracial (with one African-American and one White parent). Another generation of "beige babies!" So, how do "beige babies" help us? They may be able to identify with more than one group, and may be able to bridge racial, cultural, or language differences. They increase awareness for more mono-cultural communities of the multicultural nation and world in which we live. They may even be able to share hair-care and fashion tips with their friends from different cultures.

Many people have asked our children and other multiracial people "So, what are you anyway?" Each person may have a different answer, based on his or her own experiences. In this country, it used to be that biracial people didn't get to identify that way, but were assigned to the category that was not White. That concept, at least for individuals of mixed African ancestry, was called the "one drop rule," as in: "One drop of Black blood made you Black."

Nowadays, many people choose the race they want to identify with or choose to celebrate their multiracial heritage. Even the policies of the official United States census have reflected changing trends. The census has collected data about race since the first census in 1790. But the method of identifying race and the categories used have changed over time. Until 1960, official census-takers decided which category to put somebody into; and categories were assigned through a combination of direct interview and self-identification in 1960 and 1970. Since 1980, people have been able to select a category for themselves. And in 2000, for the first time, individuals could pick more than one race.

You might be surprised to learn that only 2.4 percent of the population had reported two or more races in 2000. Researchers have shown that many more people have mixed racial ancestry including some people who identify themselves as White.

There are many reasons why people may choose to identify with just one group; perhaps to feel closer to that community, to honor a particular aspect of their heritage, or to influence policy decisions. Some people may have selected only one race on the census form because after years of following instructions to "check only one box," they didn't feel comfortable doing anything else.

However, that may be changing. People under the age of 18 were more likely to report more than one race in the 2000 census. Forty-one percent of people who selected more than one race were under the age of 18, while just 26 percent of the total population were under age 18. Today, many kids have heroes who have a multiethnic background, such as Barack Obama and Tiger Woods. In addition to showing us a picture of opportunity, hard work, or success in their fields, they can teach us about different cultures and about the bridging role that multiethnic people can play.

A wonderful children's book, ***All the Colors of the Earth*** by Sheila Hamanaka *(HarperCollins)* says it well:

Children come in all the colors of the earth—
The roaring browns of bears and soaring eagles,
The whispering golds of late summer grasses,
And crackling russets of fallen leaves,
The tinkling pinks of tiny seashells by the rumbling sea…
Children come in all the colors of love,
In endless shades of you and me…
Children come in all the colors of the earth and sky and sea.

Here is to our wonderful, multi-hued country!

On Racial Identity in Children

Growing up in a racially and culturally diverse community helps children develop a healthy racial identity. While "race" is not determined strictly biologically, people with different physical features, including different skin colors, are sometimes treated differently. Understanding how these differences affect how we think about ourselves and others is called "racial identity development." One way to think about racial identity is these four levels: I'm OK, You're OK; Something is Not OK; I'm OK, I am not so sure about you; and I'm OK, You're OK, We're OK.

In the first level, people try to ignore that skin color makes a difference in how people are treated. It is called being "Color Blind." It would be nice if that worked, if we could truly treat all people the same way. However, there are biases built into the advertisements we see, the images on television, and in the minds of people who hire others for some jobs. For example, when I was six years old, my family quietly moved into an all-white, mostly Jewish neighborhood. Despite an act of overt racism—one morning my father had seen "N——— go back to where you came from" scrawled on the outside of the house and, without telling anyone, washed it off—my parents had hoped that the school personnel would treat me like any other child. Perhaps pretending there was no difference would allow me to "fit in." My parents hoped that an "I'm OK, you're OK" attitude would be enough to ensure my safety and success.

Unfortunately, this did not happen, for race and culture did matter. I experienced being different even as I worked to fit in. For example, during a Jewish holiday, only two students attended school, and I was the only child in my classroom. I wondered, "Why isn't the teacher teaching me today? I am here!" Both in school and socially, I was often alone. This is an example of "something is not OK."

My phase, "Something is not OK," slowly progressed to anger and the "I'm OK, I'm not sure about you" stage. One day my mother came to pick me up early from second grade because the teacher said I waited at the door and stomped on the toes of my classmates as they left the classroom! My mother observed this.

The next year my family moved from our East Coast urban area to a West Coast suburb. My new school was as culturally diverse as any Los Angeles school could offer. Miss Thomas's room was a secure and healthy place for my own emotions and my classmates' toes. I was learning about my own culture alongside many others.

My teacher used strategies that validated every child. Each day, Miss Thomas wrote a Spanish phrase in the corner of the blackboard. She read it to the class, then had the children repeat it. In less than a minute of classroom time, she acknowledged her Mexican American students and opened the door to another language for all her students. Her classroom was safe from disrespect toward her or among students. In this situation, as a result of a caring and skillful teacher, I entered into the "I'm OK, you're OK, we're OK" stage.

Understanding that each of us, whatever the color of our skin, moves through these levels in some manner may help us to accept and get along well with people with many kinds of differences.

Photo: Nana Jean's Fifth Grade Class in Los Angeles. Jean is near the middle of the middle row.

"Blink of the Eye" Racism

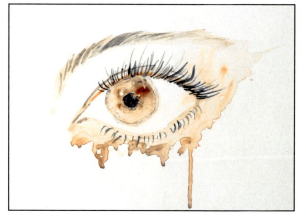

In the blink of an eye, an unintentional bias was visible to me, an African American woman. A man saw my face as I walked into a store and reached his hand back to see if his wallet was safely in his pocket. On the street a woman catches my eye a half block away and moves her purse from the handle of her baby's stroller to her side as she arranges the baby's blanket. What is happening here? Was it the sight of my brown face that caused these reactions?

I believe these are cases of "blink of the eye" racism: reactions resulting from unconscious negative feelings based on the color of skin. I don't believe it is possible to be raised in America without some feelings like this towards black or brown folks of any age. We usually do not personally choose these ways of seeing people. In fact we are usually not aware that we have such images in our heads. Such embedded feelings towards brown people seem to be in the air we breathe (not to mention the radio and TV waves). How sad, for we know that most people do not want to be considered capable of acting like this. How does it happen?

Racism and biases are rooted in stereotypes and prejudices. A stereotype is a simple image or twisted truth about a person or group based on a prior judgment of ways people act or their habits and abilities. Ethnic and racial stereotypes are learned as part of how and where we are brought up. A good example of this is a recent conversation that repeated a doll study from 1954. In a video taken in 2006 by a 17-year-old film student, a young Black child describes a Black doll as looking "bad" and the White doll as "nice."

Children are a little less able to hide these different feelings about skin color. Sometimes, even when we say, "some of my best friends are Black," we may mean that "my best friend" is an exception to stereotypes and, therefore, other Blacks would *not* be my friends.

It is important to remember that we are meant to quickly figure out who is an enemy, and who is a friend. In the past—and certainly in many places in the world today—the ability to quickly identify friend or enemy may be a matter of life or death. People who respond to their gut reactions to my brown skin in obvious, nonverbal ways may be quite gracious, if given another second or two. Recent brain research shows that while most people have an instant activity in the "fight or flight" part of their brains upon encountering an unexpected person or situation, a first reaction is often overridden in a nanosecond, allowing people to respond as their better, kind and accepting selves by overcoming built-in biases.

The first evidence of this unconscious bias came from studies categorizing insects and flowers. Dr. Anthony Greenwald drew up a list of 25 insect names and 25 flower names and found that is was far easier to place the flowers in groups with pleasant words and insects in groups with unpleasant words rather than the reverse. It was difficult to hold a mental picture of insects with words such as 'dream,' 'candy,' and 'heaven,' and flowers with words such as 'evil,' 'poison' and 'devil.' Greenwald then took the next step, using White-sounding names such as Adam and Emily and Black-sounding names such as Jamal and Latisha, and grouping them with pleasant and unpleasant words. Greenwald said that he had much more trouble putting African American names next to pleasant words than he did putting insect names with pleasant words.

Knowing that you have a feeling for or against a group may cause you to more carefully consider your responses and actions. How do we find a key to unlock this door to the mind? The Implicit Association Test, or I.A.T., is a test that has helped millions of people find out more about themselves. The **Teaching Tolerance** web site below can also help you to understand some of the words I have used: www.tolerance.org/activity/test_yourself_hidden_bias.

For an in-depth version of this, see Jean Moule's article in **Phi Delta Kappan,** *Vol. 90, no.5, Jan. 2009 (pp.320-326). Also available on her website.*

Understanding Bicultural Children

Onlooker: "That baby looks half and half."

Baby's thoughts: "That's me: half mommy and half daddy."

There was no formal category for counting individuals of multiple racial categories in the 1990 U.S. census. The 2000 U.S. census—the first to inquire about multiracial backgrounds—found that 6.8 million people, or 2.4 percent of the population, identified as multiracial.

Biracial children are one of the fastest growing populations in the United States, currently about 7 percent increase each year. This number will increase, as 1 in 7 newlywed couples are interracial. Here is the 2010 data from the census bureau:

Married Couples in the U.S. in 2010

	White Husband	Black Husband	Asian Husband	Other Husband
White Wife	50,410,000	390,000	219,000	488,000
Black Wife	168,000	4,072,000	9,000	18,000
Asian Wife	529,000	39,000	2,855,000	37,000
Other Wife	487,000	66,000	28,000	568,000

Although Children of Color eventually face some realities of a racially-charged social environment, bicultural children additionally come to understand their parents' racial drama and the perpetually repeated question, "What are you?" The interracial child represents not only the parents' racial differences but also a unique individual who must work through very personal identity issues. In many ways, the racial-identity process parallels that of monoethnic children, but with the added task of simultaneously exploring two (or more) ethnic heritages, and then integrating them into a unique identity. Perhaps the key point to remember in parenting and grandparenting biracial and multiracial children is that, psychologically, they are not merely reflections of their two or more sides but rather unique integrations of them.

On average, biracial children develop awareness of race and racial differences earlier than monoethnic children. This is because they are exposed to such differences from birth in the intimacy of their own families. It is also likely that their parents are more attuned to these differences because of their own interracial relationships. Biracial children are confronted with questions that serve as major stimuli for their internal processing of "What are you?" Concurrently, they begin to experiment with labels for themselves. Children may create descriptions based on perceptions of their skin color (such as "coffee and cream") or adopt parental terms (such as "interracial").

Biracial children have four possible options for their identity:

1) Accept the racial identity given by society;
2) Identity with the Parent of Color;
3) Identity as White if the physical features allow;
4) Identity as biracial or multiracial (no individual race identified).

Any of these choices can be positive if the choice is freely made and the individual does not feel marginalized by the choice. Biracial children should be encouraged to identify themselves differently in different situations, differently than brothers and sisters, and most importantly, differently than strangers expect them to identify.

Generally, biracial children are more successful moving through the identity formation process when race is openly discussed at home and parents and other family members are available to help them sort out the various issues of self-definition. Their rate of development also depends on the amount of integration in their communities and the role models from their two cultural sides.

During pre-adolescence, children begin to regularly use racial or cultural as opposed to physical descriptions of themselves. They become increasingly aware of group differences other than skin color (physical features, language, and so on) and of the fact that their parents belong to distinct ethnic groups. Exposure to racial incidents and first-time entry into either integrated or segregated school settings also accelerate learning.

Adolescence is particularly challenging for bicultural children. It is a time of marked intolerance for differences. There are likely to be strong pressures on bicultural adolescents to identify with one parent's ethnicity over the other—usually with the Parent of Color if one of the parents is White.

Peers of Color may push the adolescent to identify with them, and Whites may perceive and treat the bicultural adolescent as a Person of Color. Identification with one ethnic side and the simultaneous rejection of the other and then identification with the other ethnic side is a natural part of identity formation in bicultural youth.

Dating frequently begins in adolescence, which accentuates race as a central life issue. It is not unusual for biracial youth to experience romantic rejection because of their color or ethnicity, and such experiences are likely to have a great impact on their emerging sense of identity.

Biracial women have a particularly difficult task meshing their body images with the differences in physical appearance of their two parents. Young Black women often opt out of the mainstream society's beauty contests. They may find themselves so far from White America's standard of beauty that they sometimes do not even try to emulate that image and, as a result, may pursue a healthier, more realistic self-image. Biracial women can also be torn between ideal mainstream images as portrayed in the media and identification with the body image type of a Mother of Color. The heightened sexuality of adolescence also stimulates questions such as: if one becomes pregnant or makes someone pregnant, "What will the baby look like?"

Interactions between bicultural children, and their parents and grandparents are at times complex and conflicted. As children mature and become more aware, they may struggle to make sense out of how the world is reacting to them. Parents may have a difficult time understanding what their children are going through. The parents' growing realization that the child is really not like either parent but something beyond both can rouse anxiety in both parents and child, and yet this very same factor may result in the earlier mentioned independence and strong self-image.

Intercultural adoption is a second source of bicultural families. Some people in Communities of Color, especially African Americans and Native Americans, have taken strong stances against adoption and foster care across racial lines. Their feeling is that European Americans are not capable of providing ethnic children with adequate exposure and connection with their cultures of birth, or training them how to deal with the racism they will inevitably experience. While serious efforts have been made to sensitize and train adoptive parents in cultural competence as well as to encourage them to keep their children connected to the ethnic community of origin, sincere questions remain about whether such efforts can overcome the cultural gaps—like styling hair—let alone a racially-charged social environment.

White adoptive parents seldom understand the enormous difficulties that their children face as People of Color. In addition, they often unconsciously deny differences between themselves and their children.

This puts adoptive children in a difficult psychological position. They may feel isolated in dealing with the very complex issues of race and ethnicity. Often, there is a sense of disconnect caused by the gulf between how they are treated in the world and loved and treated at home. Finally, adopted Children of Color can feel confused when their adoptive parents simultaneously represent nurturance and emotional support on one side and lack of perspective and understanding on the other. My hope is that the writings in this book spark increased understanding.

—Edited excerpts from *Cultural Competence: A Primer for Educators* by Jean Moule, is a basic textbook for effective, cross-cultural teaching *(Wadsworth/Cengage Learning, 2012).*

Encouraging Passionate Pursuits

What opens the doors for passions and interests? Does environment and opportunity matter? In this section we explore elements that lead to lifelong learning and passionate pursuits.

A Letter about My Friend's Surrogate Grandchildren

Dear Jean,

You have been a dear friend of 20 years and a wonderful example of a loving wife, daughter, mother, and grandmother. I have been warmly welcomed into your extended family and made to feel much more than a colleague and friend. So I was thrilled to be asked to write a brief introduction on passionate pursuits. I decided to focus on the passionate pursuits of curious cousins, your four grandchildren that were born in a two-and-a-half-year span.

Two cousins call New York City home, a third lives in Portland, Oregon, and the fourth has moved from Tampa to San Francisco and now to Kauai, Hawaii. Nana and Pops' Cousins Camps have been an annual meeting location for the past ten years. I have been privileged to enjoy portions of each of the annual Cousins Camps, from the first Bunnies Camp (cousins at ages 3 and 1) to the latest Blood and Guts Camp (cousins at ages 12 and 10). What three constants have I noticed that underlie the Cousins Camps? Curiosity, personal choice, and caring, which are also elements that I see as leading to lifelong passionate pursuits.

Combining the freedom to explore and play in a country environment with an annual theme that includes multiple field trips, you have been encouraging the cousins to ask and find answers to their questions about bunnies, dinosaurs, frogs and amphibians, sea creatures, birds, reptiles, insects and arachnids, plants, germs, and the human body. "What is it? Why? What if? and how will we show (off) what we learned to family, friends, and neighbors at the end of camp?" were questions that drove their curiosity and creativity. The cousins dove into preparations for their play, creating costumes and props; painting backdrops, writing and rehearsing songs, dances, jokes, and quizzes for the audience; and creating illustrated programs listing the actors and narrators, and naming the various acts. As each year passed, the production has grown increasingly sophisticated, while still imbued with fun and childish humor.

Summers for the cousins have included one to three weeks of reading books cuddled with Pops in the recliner, Nana on the sofa, or lost in the pleasure of reading solo; picking blueberries and blackberries for breakfast; helping with kitchen, clean-up, and bed-making duties; hiking together in the woods and meadows; swimming in pools and lakes and trips to the ocean; participating in local track and field meets and soccer camps; and going to the Oregon State Fair. The cousins have been surrounded by the love and caring of Nana and Pops, which adds to that of their parents, other grandparents, and great-grandparents. Your grandchildren, Jean and Robbie, are loved unconditionally, allowed to explore, learn, and play to develop their curiosity, encouraged to follow their interests and talents, and given responsibilities that ensure their confidence, as all children deserve. It is a privilege and pleasure to watch them grow and develop their own personal passionate pursuits.

Bonnie

Photo: Bonnie Morihara, with Jamie and Ainsley

Nana Jean: Encouraging Passionate Pursuits

When my children were the age of my grandchildren, a woman asked me, "What are their gifts?" At the time I did not know what to say, as I knew she was looking for a gift in music, art, dance, leadership, or a passion for some facet of nature. I felt a little uncomfortable telling my new acquaintance that my children like to read, play Legos, and talk. The reader became a lawyer, the Lego player an engineer, and the talker a socially gifted teacher. Along the way, these passionate pursuits led to college majors and activities in line with their earliest interests. While many people eventually follow their *passion* in their life choices or play, many follow a more *practical* path in preparing for a career.

As an example, I pursued teaching as a career and have come only recently to following an early passion, drawing. I was aware of how I used my art background and aesthetic perceptions in everything from remodeling and garden designs to home decorating, yet a return to simple drawing has been extremely satisfying.

How have my children followed their early paths and how might my grandchildren follow theirs? In reading these connections do you see how your own path or those you care for may develop into a career that incorporates passionate pursuits?

My daughter, who read endlessly and climbed high up trees at age 5, was a competitive cyclist in college, while reading to her heart's content for a double major in English and history. She eventually completed a law degree and now climbs the subway steps in her urban environment and mountain trails when she can get away.

My son the Lego boy studied architecture and engineering in college and turned his active sports life into adventure racing and travel as he works as an engineering consultant in the USA and around the world. He continues to put together ideas and plans for the best of bicycle and pedestrian pathways.

My youngest son, the only child I know who did not go through a *No Strangers* stage around the age of one, could bring together a party in an hour as a teenager and does the same as an adult at his welcoming home. As a teacher, he leads middle school students and adults into amazing learning experiences.

And how have these gifts been transformed through connections with their life partners in the lives of the grandchildren?

My lawyer daughter married a socially-connected, precise individual with an extraordinary ear for language and music. I see their offspring having early gifts and passions that reflect this combination: both are bilingual and sing. The oldest has an eye for design, reads voluminously and revels in her athletic pursuits; the youngest connects many dots and ideas, while already showing strong leadership ability.

My engineer son married a woman with an eye for beauty and a strong sense of self. Their son is confident and already a strong cyclist at age 6. He had taken over 125 airplane flights by the time he turned 5.

The spouse of my teacher son has multiple gifts in music, drama, and leadership, as well as an ability to help others connect to what they need. Their son is off to engineering school, fluent in Spanish and especially kind to others. Their eldest daughter is already developing her artistic gifts and using them to perform. Their youngest daughter is learning Spanish, singing and of course, has Popsie (her grandfather) wrapped around her little finger. Her social gifts, reflecting both parents, began emerging in kindergarten.

Finding and Recognizing Gifts in Each

As an activity for yourself and those around you, why not make a list of your friends, family members, and classmates, and begin to list the gifts in each? Your list may begin with easily recognized ones: expertise in some area, gifts in fine or performing arts, noted leadership, creativity or the ability to make and connect friends. Consider character qualities such as dependability and flexibility or personality traits such as those who "love a challenge," or "ask deep questions."

The term "gifted" implies both giving and receiving and recognizes that the gifted person did nothing to earn it. Receiving a freely given gift may lead to a graciously accepted responsibility. Shouldn't gifts be used willingly in kindness and consideration of others? And shouldn't we have a willingness to share such gifts with the larger community?

Using Your Gifts as a Way to Make New Friends

Nana Jean began an odyssey on a ship with over 300 people including 26 who wanted to explore ancient civilizations together. So many strangers, so many times of sitting together for meals or walking together through ancient ruins. How to make friends and share our new environment? How like entering a new neighborhood or school! I wondered as I looked around who would have the same interests as I do. Who might become a long-term friend?

While I have many stories to tell, some funny, some sad, the very first thing I did was to ask questions, comment on our environment, and begin to know others as unique individuals. As I was admiring a sunset I said to a woman standing next to me that it would be fun to paint it. The very next day she and I sat on a balcony on our ship overlooking the sea and together painted water, islands, and clouds.

I discovered that my new friend and I like to play the same games and we even have matching jewelry. By asking questions of each other instead of talking about ourselves first we found much in common.

We connected with another new friend at the beginning of our journey when we visited a city new and strange to us. The calls to prayer at different times of day echo off the buildings in Istanbul, Turkey and are a regular reminder of the variety of human faith traditions in our world. This city of 14 million people has Muslim minarets and Christian churches.

In this vast city of strangers we extended our web of friends when we met a new friend through an old friend. She invited us to visit her home with a view over this city that has been inhabited for over 7,000 years. Because she has lived there for years she knew of a small place where we could eat homemade Turkish food. Allowing our new friend to lead us gave us insights into culture and tastes of exciting new foods.

Some of my favorite adventures have been when I have followed a new friend into new territory. And I enjoy showing my part of the world to others as well.

Whether a location or a skill, giving or receiving, new places and shared gifts are an excellent way to build friendships. As a guide to recognizing gifts of interpersonal relationships or skills such as art, I have a way to talk about gifts that I call Multicultural/Multi-intelligent.

There are four items listed in each of the eight intelligences in the boxed inset. Rank yourselves from low to high (1 to 5) for each gift. Which ones do you have? Which of your strengths can you share with others to make friends?

Consider making a list of the gifts you feel most comfortable sharing with others.

Discover Your Multicultural/Multi-intelligent Gifts

Visual/Spatial: Learns best by watching, Reading/using maps, Drawing, Building things

Bodily/Kinesthetic: Likes to move, Learns best by touch, Uses lots of body language, Making things by hand

Musical/Rhythmic: Listening to music, Singing/making music, Recognizing voices, Dancing/making rhythms

Verbal/Linguistic: Reading books, Telling stories/speaking, Writing/writing stories, Easily learns languages

Logical/Mathematical: Organizing things, Giving/following directions, Playing strategy games, Math/problem Solving

Interpersonal: Helping others, Works well in groups, Making new friends, Spending time with family

Intrapersonal: Valuing quiet times, Reflecting on experiences, Journaling/reflecting on self, Knowing own cultural identity

Naturalist: Appreciating nature, Prefers outdoors to in, Caring for pets/animals, Observing plant behavior

Expanding Horizons with Nana Jean!

"…gee, I'm really happy I'm so far from town." This last line from a verse in a "Music Together" song speaks to our need to get out of the city and see a bit more of the horizon. I am reminded of an essay, "Are you Rich, Are you Poor?" In this essay, a father took his son to visit a rural family in hopes that he would see poverty. Instead the son came home with a few reflections like this: "I saw that we have one dog and they have four. We have a pool that reaches to the middle of our garden and they have a creek that has no end. Our patio reaches only to the front yard and they have the whole horizon. We buy our food from supermarkets, but they grow theirs. We have walls around our property to protect us; they have friends to protect them." The boy's father was speechless. Then his son added, "Thanks, Dad, for showing me how poor we are."

Ainsley, 5, and Jamie, 3, playing by our small pond.

Two of my grandchildren live in Manhattan, and they could use some of those expanded horizons. When shown a book with photos of New York City from the air they could easily identify Central Park, Metropolitan Museum of Art, Battery Park, Museum of Natural History and my favorite: "That's the Chrysler building near my Daddy's office!" But could they throw rocks in a river, or identify edible berries? In late June Jamie, 3, and Ainsley, 5, were without a babysitter, and their Mommy and Daddy decided that two months with Nana Jean and Pops, who live on four acres in rural Oregon, was a good solution.

We live on a ridge overlooking farms and forests, and while there is much to do, the children particularly *love* our small ponds. One day Jamie and I were walking around the ponds watching little "skitter bugs" darting around on the surface of the water. I told Jamie we needed a frog in the pond to eat those bugs. The next day I heard him talking to his older sister Ainsley as he looked at all of those bugs. He said, "Nana needs a **big** frog."

We were surprised to find that the mosquito fish had survived the winter, so we had an exciting time looking for them in the water and trying to count them. One day we decided to buy 40 goldfish for five dollars. Ainsley correctly suggested that we "release" the fish into the three ponds. Ainsley had to do the math on how to divide them. I think we decided on eight in each of the small ones and fourteen in the large one…wait, that is only 30…hmm…no wonder there were more than we thought! We put 39 goldfish in the ponds…the 40th did not even survive the ride home: he/she was duly buried, dug up and buried again…now with a marker on the island in the ponds. So, the children, as well as the two cats, spend much time looking into the water…where were those fish hiding?

One day they built a sand castle on the sand island in the ponds. Yes, the island has become a sandbox… not something I had planned on, but they were happy. The children helped to remove the algae that grew on the surface. Once, Jamie caught and released a goldfish. Some days the children went from PJs to swimsuit to PJs as they played in the sand, water and sun.

After getting tanned, with tough feet and lots of learning about gardening and llamas and forests and fish, Ainsley and Jamie flew home. As the last line of the song goes, "…gee, I'm really happy I'm back home in town."

Nana Jean: Cousins' Country Camp

Of the four grandchildren (from our three children) the oldest just turned 8, and the other three are very close in age—5, 6 and 6. They have lived very far away from each other: Florida, New York and Oregon. Because one of them is an only child and one has much older siblings, they really do appreciate spending time together as cousins. While holidays are fun, that usually only happens once a year…so Nana *(also known as Nannie)* and Pops *(also known as Popsie)*, decided to have a Cousins' Camp. *(Photo below shows the kids in their "Bird Camp" outfits singing a Chinese song).*

Each year, we have tried to match the focus of the camp with the ages of our grandchildren. We started with bunnies when the three youngest were around age one and moved to frogs when they were two. When they were three years old, our theme was dinosaurs, then birds when they were four, and last year we chose insects as our theme. This summer the theme will be "sea creatures."

Each year, a seamstress makes them matching outfits: twirly skirts for the girls, reversible short pants for the boys, and t-shirts with the theme item on it. The camps used to be about four days long in the beginning and now they may be as long as three weeks.

We try to:

• See the actual creatures alive (for dinosaurs, there were very life-like creatures at a zoo exhibit). During the camps over the years, we have gone to see bunnies at the feed store, frogs around a lake where we hiked, and dinosaurs moving and roaring at the zoo exhibit. When we had the bird theme, we visited a nearby zoo where a Lorikeet exhibit allowed the children to feed the birds. We also had bird identification books with sounds for all the birds seen wherever we were. For insect camp, we had three weeks: the first week was about insects in general and we had two books to identify anything that we caught. The second week, we studied and looked for arachnids, and the third week we had emerging butterflies in a butterfly hatching kit.

• Find local camps that are related to the theme. For instance, at the local children's museum we found day camps on frogs and butterflies. Other things are worked in because they are available and we make them fit: an art camp, trips to the ocean, camping and hiking, and crafts, lots of crafts.

• Most years the children also work on a Cousins' Camp Production. This involves writing a skit, making costumes or parts of sets, choreographing, making and giving out programs.

Over time, my adult children have arranged their own vacations as couples during our Cousins' Camp when they know their children will be happily engaged.

Children spend many hours with Popsie in his garden, helping to plant, weed, water, pick, wash, cut, and prepare fresh veggies, and of course, eat them! Every year, after the first time picking them, Chance wanted to dig up potatoes a second time. He also wanted to gather onions. They all love to pick berries.

The cousins who have been in Oregon in spring or early summer have helped in planting. Bella has planted onions, and Ainsley and Jamie, corn.

Pops says: "When they are here in the summer they can see the progress of what they have planted earlier. If they are here late enough, they can help harvest and eat."

The children have learned about and enjoyed natural foods and the enjoyment of gardening as well. Healthy memories!

Learning by Working Together

Do you learn by having people tell you what to do? Or, do you learn from watching? I learned from my granddaughter how easy it is to gain skills and get information simply from working together with others.

A few years ago a former teacher of my children invited us to take part in a garden tour that raised money to help to restore a beautiful old house in our community. Not considering myself a true gardener and dreading the thought of getting ready for a couple of hundred people to walk on our property, I said no. After repeated requests, I finally agreed.

There is very little in life that will get one planning, working, and gardening as much as being part of a garden tour. Almost everything else going on in my life was not as important as preparing for the tour, and my answer to any requests for other activities became, "Not now, maybe in July, after the garden tour."

One exception was when our son asked us to have our granddaughter, Bella, for the week before the tour. At age 7, she helps more and needs less supervision. I learned an incredible lesson: my passion and depth of commitment for this tour translated effortlessly to her. Her mother later said that after one week she seemed more mature. At the beginning of the week she cried and asked for her mother; but by the end of the week she confidently showed her mother and brother around when they arrived for the tour. She took them to the 20 stops on the walk around our place, showing them how we have a naturescape, which means that as we look at the plants and trees that grow naturally in this area, we encourage some, remove some, and add some.

She not only learned how to transplant tiny plants and memorized the common and Latin names of some plants, but also helped me note the tiny, identifiable flowers on native plants that had found homes on our land. Her questions and comments as the native plant experts came to help us identify green things encouraged us all.

Her hands and legs saved mine as she ran to get tools and materials. She hauled buckets of weeds and dirt from the molehills that appeared each morning.

Bella likes to draw and letter. During the week she made the cutest signs, like one that hung on a high fence we called "Woodhenge." As people entered our property they laughed as they read her sign: *"Phlox: inside fence = nice phlox, outside fence = deer-eaten phlox."* Most of her signs were ones of caution: signs that said, *"Cats and Frogs Only"* kept people off some delicate bridges and walkways near our pond. And she helped me feel better about the dandelions I did not remove near one of the fences: *"WARNING! Do not pick dandelions, llamas will stick their heads out to eat them."*

"I have lots to do," she said before the tour began. She helped people find their way around, and she sold both her own and other people's plants at "Bella's Boutique." By the middle of the day she spoke of her fellow vendors as co-workers, referring visitors to them as needed and explaining what she was selling. She learned to smile, to share and to encourage others to take some of the plants home to their own gardens.

While I doubt that she will remember the Latin name of a dandelion, at least she knows it has one. She learned that plants need to move to larger containers as she saw the root-bound small tree she helped me replant. She knows that a smile and nice presentation will help sell goods. And she knows how much work goes on behind the scenes for such a tour. She learned by watching and working alongside of her "Nannie" and "Popsie," as she calls us.

Bella, instead of being a drag on my time, was the highlight of our tour and my most precious and wonderful memory of the day.

On Geocaching

My granddaughter Bella turned ten on a recent Saturday. For her party her mother arranged a food crawl on a street near their house in Portland, Oregon. As we were walking, I remembered a similar walk on this street to find geocaches.

Geocaching is a worldwide treasure hunt based on satellites circling our globe. It was invented in Oregon about 15 years ago.

A Global Positioning System (GPS) gives the latitude and longitude coordinates that allow geocaches to be found. The GPS, a space-based satellite navigation system, provides location and time information in all weather conditions, anywhere on or near the earth where there is an unobstructed line of sight to four or more GPS satellites. The United States government created the system, maintains it, and makes it freely accessible to anyone with a GPS receiver. Many smart phones include a GPS system and inexpensive phone apps can connect to the geocaching site on the web.

The geocaching site gives information on the location and details for caches, including what size they are and hints to find them. A typical cache is a small waterproof container that contains a logbook with a pen or pencil. Geocachers enter the date they found it and sign it with their established geocaching code name. After signing the log, the cache must be placed back exactly where it was found. Many caches have trinkets that can be taken in trade for another item.

Caches are hidden by other geocachers and there are millions of caches around the world, including one on the space station. Each cache is given attributes by the owner to let other geocachers know, for example, whether it is a good one for children or what facilities or obstacles may be near by. Other examples of the many attributes are: wheelchair-accessible, requires wading to get to, easy to bicycle to, has a picnic table. The owner may also let geocachers know if it is accesible all hours or has scenic views.

Bella and I went geocaching recently. She found a cache in a camouflaged container by a bridge and a very small cache hidden in a vine on a street corner.

My own favorite series of caches were the ones I located when I trekked on Mt. Kilimanjaro. A cache was located near each of the huts where I spent the nights. There was a *Virtual Cache* at the summit, and a regular cache on the edge of the crater at the top.

Each cache has a number that rates the terrain from 1 to 5, as well as how difficult it is to find it from 1 to 5. The cache on Mt. Kili was a 5/5.

A *Virtual Cache* is one that requires the geocacher to tell the owner something about the site online. There is no physical cache. There are also *Earth Caches* that give information about geological features and require the finder to answer questions about the location.

Some caches, called *Multi-Caches,* are placed as part of a series, and require the geocacher to find one cache, so they can get the coordinates to the next one and so on. *Challenge, Mystery,* or *Puzzle Caches* require the finder to solve a puzzle to find the coordinates for the next cache location. Some *Challenge Caches* may require a city tour or exploration of a garden or art exhibit.

Other *Challenge Caches* may require you to do some caching adventure before you can find the final cache. I have completed two challenges. One was to find a cache every day of the year, and the ABC Challenge that requires you to find 26 caches whose titles begin with each letter of the alphabet. Another difficult challenge I completed was to find *Lonely Caches*, which have not been found by anyone for a year or more.

The variations are endless, and the creativity of the cachers who hide caches continues to amaze me.

I started geocaching because my son was a geocacher, and I accidentally found a cache. Since then, I have found over 3,400 caches, many with my grandchildren. Not only have I happened upon others looking for a cache at the same time I was, but I have had caching adventures with friends, and made new friends.

Geocachers often plan events where cachers get together to talk about geocaching and explore a particular area. During events called *CITO* or *Cache In, Trash Out,* geocachers help clean up an area.

Events all over the world, including some mega events with thousands of participants, give geocachers an opportunity to meet others living in a different state or country. *Visit geocaching.com. The membership is free.*

—Jean Moule, PhD, author, artist and geocacher, Oregon.

Cultivating Focused Human Beings

While each of us is born into and becomes part of a culture, language and place, within those parts of our lives are many different opportunities that help us become unique individuals with unique contributions to our local and global communities.

I help my grandchildren make their way in the world with their passions through what I call the "Eight-Year-Old Trip." As each of my four grandchildren hit age 8, I identify some great and wonderful interest of theirs and take them on a trip to explore it.

Jamie at the Vivero (hatchery)

By helping each one of my grandchildren become immersed in one of their interests, I hope to broaden their understanding. I also hope to give them viewpoints and language (both technically and linguistically speaking) that will help them pursue those interests as they grow.

When Ainsley turned 8, she had read J.K. Rowlings' series multiple times. The *Wizarding World of Harry Potter* had just opened at Universal Studios in Orlando, Florida. I flew from Oregon to New York City to pick her up, and we enjoyed three days of just Nana and Ainsley time. What a revelation! With only one youngster as a focus, we ate when she wanted to eat and did what she wanted to do! She grew up a lot in those three days: very little whining, and her clear requests were answered by me with a **yes**.

After Ainsley's trip, I began to wonder how to bond with and support Jamie. Jamie has talked about turtle conservation since age 4. Would his parents allow me to take him out of the country for **his** 8-year trip? Where could we go? His mother found reasonable airfares from NYC to Costa Rica. And we were off: first to find a suitable project, and then to make detailed plans.

We ended up on the Nicoya Peninsula at the *Refugio Mixta del Vida Silvestre Romelia,* near Montezuma, an organization that protects Olive Ridley sea turtles as they hatch and crawl to the sea. It was an adventure into Jamie's interest and also into a unique surrounding culture. We used my very limited Spanish and his better Spanish to navigate the area and work through unexpected situations that arose.

Here is an example from my journal:

"Jamie and I are sitting at the hatchery *(vivero)* at 9:20 AM, 50 minutes into our 2 ½ hour shift. Fidel and Eoghan left, tired. They had been exhuming nests and digging the dirt out. The nests will air out for a day and then clean sand will be added in preparation for a new nest. When they were exhuming the nests, they found 21 little turtles. We watched two that were just coming out of the shell to complete their hatching. We knew the turtles probably would not survive or get to the surface without our help. There was one little hatchling that we had to help just a bit at the beginning of its slow but steady crawl towards the sea. As the water reached it, and it started to swim away with one flipper poking up on a stroke. Jamie said, 'He waved goodbye to us.' Another time, as three turtles that he had named swam away, he said, 'Good life, Jamie! Good life, Fidel! Good life, Bob!'"

This trip certainly ranks as one of the top ten weeks of my life, and I am certain Jamie will never forget it either. One of the other workers on the project said, "He is ridiculously smart for his age. He knows so much. He uses many words that an eight year old shouldn't know, like *endemic* and *marsupial*. There will be something very wrong in this world if he does not become a biologist or conservationist. The world needs enthusiastic people like him."

Two grandchildren have passed age 8, and there are two more to go. Chance likes to bike, hike and climb. Perhaps a trip to Utah for canyoneering and biking? And Bella—Will it be her fluent Spanish? Ballet? Singing? People skills? We'll soon see.

On Creativity

What opens the door for passions and interests? Does environment or opportunity matter? And how are those related to talents?

I remember a teacher telling my mother that I had completed an art project extremely well. Eventually I majored in art. Now, I consider myself an artist and work to introduce my grandchildren to art and design.

Most of my own work is landscapes, trees, clouds, mountains. I have painted in the Cayman Islands, Mexico, and Hawaii. The ocean looks the same. If I were painting people and villages and images from around the world, the cultures would be evident as they are in many images in *Skipping Stones*. Perhaps one day I will. I expect my trips to Greece and Egypt will include simple landscapes that connect us across the globe.

A recent Cousins Camp theme on plants seemed like a foundation for artwork for my grandchildren. I invited my own art mentor, Paul Toews, to teach my four grandkids, Bella, Jamie, Chance, and Ainsley, how to draw and paint trees *(see photo below)*. Paul had taught *me* to paint trees and three of my works in this book were done in his class *(p. 21 and the top of p. 54)*.

By Ainsley, drawn at age 10.

We gave each child brushes, paints and paper. During two sessions the children first drew an evergreen tree and then painted a deciduous tree.

Some of the artwork remained in boxes, while Bella's parents framed and hung them on a wall not far from one of my own works.

Bella sees herself as an artist. While she is growing into her own passions in many ways, artwork continues as an interest. Recently, we worked together to paint miniature pieces of clouds and mountains. As I suggested we move to another subject she stated that she wanted to "do an abstract." Layers of paint and color later she signed the work and gave it to me as a gift.

Ainsley has a talent in design and puts together outfits for herself and Bella. She can turn a trip to a used clothing store into a fashion show.

The grandchildren have designed and floated boats, put together costumes for the Cousins Camp, and painted huge backdrops for their programs. The simplest of materials, a bit of glue, and freedom to make a mess, and they are off. Summers work because the mess stays outside. Dirty children? We can hose them off.

Some projects are fun in the making and have no purpose but play. Others are photographed and sent to parents. And some are hung with pride.

~*Jean Moule, artist, www.jeanmoule.com/creativity, Oregon.*

Nurturing Grandchildren

All parents face the task of creating a safe environment in which the child may move without harm through the developmental stages of growing up. Threats to the child's health or safety are mediated or removed by the child's parents. But Children of Color are also systematically subjected to the harmful effects of racism. Parents of Color are aware of what awaits their children and know that there is only so much they can do to protect them. What can all parents and grandparents of Children of Color do?

Families can create a buffer zone in which children are protected from the negative attitudes and stereotypes that abound in the broader society. Part of this process involves instilling a sense of ethnic pride. In such a safe environment, the child is more likely to develop a more positive sense of self. Help your grandchild build confidence by teaching them about their culture, where they come from, and family stories. Teach them to respect others' beliefs and traditions even if they may directly contradict your own.

Parents and grandparents can teach their children how to deal emotionally with the negative experiences of racism. Start to build communication early with them by making their school stories a priority. Do not get angry if they tell you a story in which they made a mistake. And parents can prepare their children for what they will encounter in the world outside the buffer zone. It is possible to help children become a part of the solution. One parent says, "I teach my kids that we are not better than, but we are just as good as anyone. I think that helps breaks the cycle of oppression."

Listening helps. How can a parent or grandparent create an environment in which a silenced child feels the confidence or security to speak? More often than not, such efforts produce results only slowly over time. Previously silenced children may require multiple opportunities based on mutual respect and trust before they feel safe enough to express what is on their minds and in their hearts.

All young children must be protected and nurtured until they are able to venture forth with sufficient skills and abilities to protect themselves. Involvement in passionate pursuits, identification of individual talents, and expanded horizons of all kinds help create this safe and growing place for children.

Children of Color are often at risk, and it is especially critical for their parents and grandparents to create within them a good psychological base grounded in a strong and positive sense of self. Research has repeatedly shown that a positive self-concept is correlated with effective social functioning, higher levels of cognitive development, and greater emotional health and stability. Simple positive adventures and activities are key to this strong sense of self and place in the world. The buffer zone against racism and negative racial messages can provide a place and time for optimal personal growth. Parents and grandparents create this zone.

Children's concepts of self result directly from the messages they receive about themselves from the world. According to psychological theories about the development of the self, children take in and make a part of themselves the views of others, through a process of mirroring and reflection. If they are loved, they will love themselves; if they are demeaned or devalued, that is how they will feel about themselves and treat others. Children who are rejected begin to question whether they deserve respect from the larger society. By substituting the reflection of loving parents and grandparents for that of an often hostile environment that may routinely negate the value of children because of their ethnicity, a more positive sense of self is guaranteed. The child who is loved, accepted and supported, comes to love and to respect herself as someone worthy of love.

However, the idea of a buffer zone should not be limited merely to parents and family. Communities, particularly Communities of Color, often serve this purpose. The African adage that "it takes an entire village to raise a child" is relevant here: In many African languages, the same word is used to mean mother and aunt, and child-rearing is the responsibility of all the adults in the village.

There are many ways to help children deal emotionally with negative racial experiences. Children should not be allowed to feel alone in their struggle. They must feel the support of their parents, grandparents, peers, and teachers and also understand that they are part of a long history of People of Color who have struggled against racism. Parents should model active intervention and mastery over the environment as well as help their children develop competence and the ability to achieve personal goals. If children experience their parents as powerful, they gain a sense of vicarious power. Sometimes, children should be allowed to try to deal with racial situations on their own, with parents prepared to intervene if necessary. Other times, it is the parent's responsibility to work to resolve the situation quickly and appropriately, and above all, to protect the child's self-esteem.

At some point, children must learn to manage the righteous anger that they will feel as objects of racial hatred. Suppressing anger eventually leads to self-loathing and low self-esteem. Overgeneralized anger is counterproductive, leads nowhere, and consumes a vast amount of undirected energy. A more balanced approach seems optimal: teaching children to assert themselves sufficiently, to display their anger appropriately, and to sublimate and channel much of it into constructive energy for actively dealing with the world. *"Our job,"* Alvin Poussaint wrote, *"is to help our children develop that delicate balance between appropriate control and appropriate display of anger and aggression, love and hate."* He continued, *"As parents we must try to raise men and women who are emotionally healthy in a society that is basically racist. If our history is a lesson, we will continue to survive. Many Black children will grow up to be strong, productive adults. But too many others will succumb under the pressures of a racist environment. Salvaging these youngsters is our responsibility as parents."*

One parent, also a teacher, described this process in her home:

I don't think that creating a safe and supportive classroom environment means that you have to give students the impression that there are not challenges in life that they will encounter. As I raise my own children as African American, I try to create a home environment that is safe for them to ask questions, get angry, and express their feelings in a healthy way. I feel that this gives them a place to gain confidence in themselves as individuals and know what they believe and why they believe it. When they enter the world, they can speak with that same confidence and be able to support it.

—*Angela Freeman, February, 2010*

Equally important to providing children with a strong emotional base is preparing them for the eventual experience of prejudice and discrimination to be encountered in the broader world. How may children be prepared?

Never deny children's ethnicity or underestimate its possible impact on their lives. Some parents feel that it is best to put off such discussions as long as possible, thereby protecting children from the horror of racism until it can no longer be avoided. There are real problems with this approach. First of all, it models a denial of reality that not only confuses children but also sets them on the course of not actively dealing with their ethnicity. Parents and grandparents who choose to avoid discussions of race tend to underestimate the level of children's knowledge and may be avoiding issues that have already become real and problematic for the children.

Most ethnic children are aware of racial differences as early as two or three years of age and by seven are aware of the negative judgments that society holds about their group. Ethnic children might want and need to discuss their experiences but may feel that they must remain silent because of the family rule: "We do not talk about these things." By such tactics, parents and grandparents unintentionally remove themselves as important resources for their children.

It is clearly best to allow children to bring up the subject of race and ethnicity and to deal with it in the context of their ongoing reality. Parents and grandparents should answer questions in as simple a manner as possible and not overwhelm children with more knowledge than they need. More often than not, a small amount of information will suffice. Family members should answer questions in a manner that fits with the children's level of cognitive development. Similarly, children should not be overwhelmed emotionally with difficult information or stories. Preparing children for dealing with racism is not a single event; it is an ongoing developmental process. As they encounter racism in the real world, it should be discussed and processed; and as they mature, information and explanations should also grow in depth and comprehensiveness.

With help children may develop a strong and positive ethnic identity based on values inherent in group memberships. This identity helps the child to internally counteract the negative experiences of being an object of prejudice. Children should be able to say: "I am an African American, and I come from a rich cultural tradition of which I am proud. Sure, I experience racism, but that is just the way it is, although, at times, I get angry. But I would not trade it for being White or anything else, even if it meant life would be easier." An ethnic identity based solely on negative experiences of racial hatred is a very fragile thing that disappears as soon as the adversity is gone. If children are made to feel bad because of how they are different, it is psychologically crucial that they have and can draw on positive feelings about who they are ethnically and individually as well. If they do not, they may in time come to hate their group membership, seeing it as a source of their problems.

Racism should be presented as a social issue, not as an individual or personal problem. For example, a child might say: "Why did Tommy call me that bad name? I didn't do anything to him." A good answer might be: "Of course you didn't. Sometimes, when people get angry or unhappy, they take it out on others who are different from them. There is something wrong with people when they do that." Children must not come to believe—consciously or unconsciously—that something they did brought on the racist behavior. Parents and grandparents should not assume that a child has not personalized a negative racial experience. They should check it out. In their egocentric mode of experiencing the world, young children tend to take responsibility for most things that happen to them. Supportive family members should actively make sure they do not do so. An ethnic child can be transformed from a happy and carefree young person to one who is negative and sullen by a single experience with racism. Much of the damage could be alleviated by working through the incident with the child.

Children should learn two lessons about ethnic group membership. The first is that group membership is based not only on obvious physical or cultural features but also on an interdependence of societal pressures: Members of an ethnic group share the experience of being treated similarly by the world. This should serve to heighten awareness of being part of a single whole. But it is easy for children to learn to vent their frustration on subgroups within their community, blaming them for the bad treatment that all group members experience. Such internalized racism can become a tyranny of its own and lead to destructive intergroup struggles. For example, I am thinking of caste systems based on lightness and darkness of skin color that exist in many Communities of Color. In my own culture, there was a time when a rushee for a Black sorority was accepted based partially on whether her skin tone was lighter than a standard brown paper bag.

The second lesson is that it is acceptable to have multiple allegiances and belong to different social groupings at the same time. If children are made to choose between alternatives, they sometimes grow resentful and may eventually get even with parents, usually by rejecting group membership at some level. For example, some parents are very critical of their children's attempts at being bicultural (of trying to become competent in the ways of dominant culture as well as their own). Fearing that their children may lose touch with traditional ways and values, they force them to choose, and the result is unhappiness for all concerned. The same result may come from forcing the child to acculturate into the mainstream culture, which may engender later yearning for identity.

Parents and grandparents should realize that children's feelings about ethnicity, ethnic identity, and group belonging are not likely to be more positive or less conflicted than their own. Put in a slightly different manner, parents may pass on inner conflicts and issues about their own ethnicity to their children. In preparing children for a sometimes hostile world, parents and grandparents should focus not only on their children but also on themselves as role models.

A Letter from the Editor of Skipping Stones Magazine

Dear Jean,

This section on global customs and cultures, that you asked me to introduce, is in a way a representation of *Skipping Stones*! Each Volume takes the readers on a journey around the world—from Africa to Europe, from North America to South America and Asia. We strive to highlight the incredible global diversity of the many languages, cultures, celebrations, religions, and ways of living. We explore stewardship of the ecological and social webs that nurture us. We offer a forum for communication among children from different lands and backgrounds. **Skipping Stones** expands horizons in a playful, creative way. We aim high in our pages; we are not afraid to touch difficult subjects in the magazine.

Skipping Stones is probably one of a kind, the most multicultural magazine in the whole nation. And your column makes it more so. Almost 30 years ago, I was attending an international peace conference at a Gandhian Ashram in Western India, which was where I conceived a global education magazine for children around the world; a magazine that focused on cultural diversity and appreciation of nature and its wholesomeness, all while promoting critical thinking and creativity in children. Now, we are embarking on the 28th year of the magazine! *Skipping Stone*s continues to be a forum for children of diverse backgrounds by featuring contributions—poems, articles, letters, stories, art, and photos—by children of all ages. And each week, we mentor student interns and volunteers in our office.

Walking our talk is very important—young people learn by observing what others are doing. I speak five different languages. I have bicycled in eight different countries on three different continents, spent more than 18 months in Latin America, walked 500 miles on a peacewalk in Central America, and experienced the hospitality of dozens of cultures around the world. I admire you taking your grandkids on meaningful overseas excursions. They will surely draw on those experiences later in their lives.

In addition to working full-time on editing and publishing the magazine, I also involve myself with interfaith and social issues, nature activities, and creative and educational work. I serve on the human rights commission of the city of Eugene, Interfaith Prayer Services International, and volunteer with the Food for Lane County Youth Farm and feeding the homeless, etc. This afternoon, while writing this letter, I took time to attend a celebration of the Latin Heritage Month at the public library. Every multicultural celebration we attend enriches our lives.

When we published your very first piece in our pages, I had no idea where it would lead us. It has proved to be the beginning of a lasting professional relationship. Our meetings at the National Association for Multicultural Education's annual conferences have also been helpful in many ways. This section, like the whole book, reflects both of our passions for multicultural understandings. Thanks for involving yourself in *Skipping Stones*, and inviting us to collaborate with you.

Arun

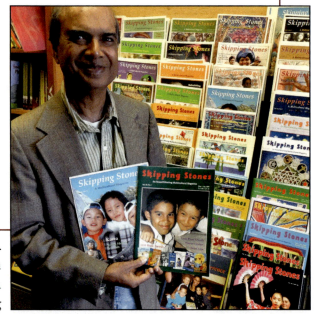

Arun Narayan Toké, executive editor Skipping Stones.
Subscriptions: Family: $25; Institutions: $35, from
Skipping Stones P.O. Box 3939, Eugene, OR 97403 USA
info@SkippingStones.org; www.SkippingStones.org

Reflections on Cultures, Customs, and Countries I have Visited

Seeing the world from different perspectives and through different eyes opens our minds to ways of knowing as well as common human understandings and relationships.

On Deep Culture

Travellers to different countries and different cultures are aware of the surface cultures they encounter. Music, clothing, dance, art, language and food catch our eyes and other senses. We come from these experiences with souvenirs and memories of these things. Yet much of culture lies beneath the surface, just as most of an iceberg lies beneath the water.

I became more aware of these differences as I visited Cristin, a former student who teaches on Cayman Brac, a lovely island in the Caribbean. Seventeen miles long and one mile wide, the island was settled first by shipwrecked sailors and then by European farmers and enslaved Africans. Many of the 1,600 Caymanians on the Brac are descendents of these settlers and share their last names. The islanders' skin colors range from ebony to ivory.

Cristin teaches music to the elementary students on Cayman Brac and has found ways to use her violin skills in the community. She saw a deep difference in the children she taught at private schools on Grand Cayman, where many of the children came from families with a lot of money and power, and those she works with in the public schools on Cayman Brac. On Grand Cayman the children were more likely to think of, and work for, themselves. On Cayman Brac Cristin works with children who seem more eager and focused on looking out for each other. This was a warm culture with deep roots in the history of the island.

People on Cayman Brac share music, musical instruments, stories, history and other "surface culture"

materials in schools, museums and community settings. I have a photo of Cristin examining an old violin in one of the exhibits. Most of these exhibits focus on the surface culture of the island while seldom showing deep culture with hidden rules and connections. These hidden parts of culture have an *emotional load*. Emotional load is the deep emotions that are connected to these hidden parts of culture. These hidden feelings touch us deeply, and we may not be aware of them at first. The ***Iceberg Concept of Culture*** explains this.

I found that the people were slow to make eye contact and to talk with me until we were introduced. An elderly resident of the island told me a couple of stories that helped me understand the way islanders interact with each other. In such a small community ways to communicate with a look might be very different and more important than talking.

Sometimes there were strong storms and hurricane winds, and sea water would come onto the island. As it doesn't have high (safe) places except for the caves, many people would gather tightly together in these caves. Because they were so close physically, they may have given themselves more space by the way they looked or did not look at each other. While so close together, they would have to pay more attention to eye contact and facial expressions. The ways in which the children play with each other, look at each other, talk to each other and, perhaps, look out for each other in both everyday and difficult situations may come from the ways their grandparents had to take care of and interact with each other many decades ago.

On my next visit, I hope to talk with teachers about the hidden cultural connections. Perhaps the students will understand more about their culture when they look at and understand the iceberg of culture.

How about you? Can you think of parts of your culture that are in the top of the iceberg above water? What parts of your culture are harder to see and are hidden under the water? Feel free to write me about your iceberg of culture: moulej@oregonstate.edu.

On New Perspectives

I recently rediscovered the value of seeing the world from a new perspective when I moved from skiing down the mountain to flying over it, while confronted with rapid changes and challenges.

I have enjoyed skiing and snowboarding with my children and friends for many years near Santiam Pass in Oregon. During my years of ski instructing and ski patrolling, I have driven over the pass many times, and I have spent hours on the top of Hoodoo Butte. From there you can see the Sand Mountain Volcanic Alignment and its gentle, rounded snow-covered slopes.

My perspective, based on my own experience and view, was transformed when I climbed into the pilot's seat of a small airplane. Suddenly, my ingrained assumptions were shattered when I saw the full picture.

When I arrived at the airport for my next flying lesson, we first had to determine: "Is it a flyable day?" or "Will the weather cooperate?" Fall and winter weather in Oregon often mean overcast skies and frequent rain. I have a shirt that says, "Oregon State Rain Festival: *January 1 to December 31.*" In the weeks before my flight, our typical autumn's cloudy skies and rains had set in, yet here was a week of clear, sunny weather, and my hopes of flying over the Cascades reawakened. I had not flown above 5,000 feet yet. With the pass at 4,800 feet, and the surrounding peaks at 10,000 feet, we would go first to 5,500, then 7,500 and then 9,500 feet as needed to help ensure safe distance from other planes and gain altitude to cross the crest of the mountains. I was excited. My instructor was willing. My husband-photographer, Rob, would go along. Before take-off, my instructor cautioned me that though the sky was clear, the winds might not be easy to handle.

As we took off and headed east, first over our four acres and then over the towns in the Santiam Canyon I knew so well, we noted the smoke from home chimneys rising straight up into the cloudless skies. Good, I thought, no wind. As we climbed higher, the tops of the Three Sisters mountains came into view. Then we noticed the snow on the peak of North Sister being blown strongly south and west.

Where did those winds come from, I wondered? But I knew that the climate in Eastern Oregon on the other side of the Cascades Range was much different. I couldn't see the winds, but I was starting to feel them.

Sure enough, as we came to the summit of Santiam Pass, the winds began to shake us up quite a bit. "I don't like this!" I said. I was approaching the summit at an angle as instructed because it is much more difficult to change direction if you are headed straight over and winds push you down. Approaching at that angle and noticing the turbulence, I easily and slowly turned us away from the crest and back into smoother air.

I was too focused on piloting the plane to look down, but as we turned, Rob took a photo of the ski area we have enjoyed for years. When we had time to look at the pictures, we discovered, to our amazement, that the Sand Mountains were actually part of a row of small craters, not smooth peaks! The view from the air opened our minds to this incredible new understanding of the terrain we had travelled and viewed for years. I had gained a valuable new perspective.

My experience of seeing the earth's features in a new way reminded me that there is often much more depth and complexity in people than we see on the surface. It's like icebergs: what may appear as a small iceberg from the sea's surface often has a large mass under water. Just as sailors have to remember to account for that unseen underwater mass, people should remember that much about other people is also unseen but vitally important. Both individuals and culture have more depth than we first realize. Most of us think of culture as food, clothing, music and art. Yet the deep customs of relationships, our understanding of time and even how much space we give each other when we stand close are equally as significant.

May the unseen winds and varying perspectives of the earth help us acknowledge the limitations of our own viewpoints and help us begin to understand the cultures and experiences of those around us.

And now I will think about those Sand Mountains differently when I ski down the slope looking at them.

—Jean Moule, student pilot, Oregon.

Aloha from the Birthplace of Our Biracial President

"You can't really understand Barack until you understand Hawai'i." —First Lady Michelle Obama

President Obama is a kama'āina, or land child, born in Hawai'i. Are there specifics in Hawai'i's culture and history that help him to be a good president? As kama'āina Obama was raised and went to school among people from different places and cultures that learned to live in harmony.

Aloha: a common greeting. It means *more* than 'Hello.' That *more* may help us to understand the deep roots of our president's outlook that may serve our diverse nation well. It was in Hawai'i that he came to believe "that our patchwork heritage is a strength, not a weakness." Obama speaks specifically of his family: "As a child of a Black man and a White woman, someone who was born in the racial melting pot of Hawai'i, with a sister who's half Indonesian…and a brother-in-law and niece of Chinese descent…I've never had the option of restricting my loyalties on the basis of race, or measuring my worth on the basis of tribe."

Aloha means giving from the heart in a respectful manner. It means mutual regard and affection, and extends warmth in caring with no obligation in return. Each person is important to all others for collective existence. Obama said, "That's why we pass on the values of empathy and kindness to our children by living them."

In the concepts below, based on the Hawai'ian language, I've included quotes from Obama to help us understand how the concepts have impacted him.

Mana: divine spirit or power that is in every person, rock and flower. Today people of all faiths live in Hawai'i side by side. Hawai'ians practice many faiths: Christian, Jewish, Muslim, Hindu, Buddhist, and Native Hawai'ian faith traditions. Obama says, "Faith is not just something you have, it is something you do."

'Aina: the land. "Growing up in Hawai'i, not only do you appreciate the natural beauty, but there is an ethic of concern for the land that dates back to native Hawai'ians."

Akahai: kindness.

'Olu'olu: agreeable. "No place else could have provided me with the environment, the climate, in which I could not only grow, but also get the sense of being loved."

Akamai: smart, clever, skilled, expert. "There is so much out there that you can be curious about and learn about." Obama says that his school "embraced me, gave me support, gave me encouragement and allowed me to grow and to prosper."

Kuleana: privilege, duty and responsibility. "Individual responsibility and mutual responsibility—that's the essence of America's promise."

Ahonui: patience, perseverance. "I want us to think about the long term and not just the short term."

Kōkua: help, aid, assist, support, helping to get something done. "If we see somebody who's in need, we should help."

Kupuna: ancestor, grandparent, respected elder. Obama explains how his grandmother took care of him and taught him so much, and her importance in his life.

Keiki: child. Everyone older is called Auntie or Uncle when you are small. And keiki are cherished by all. "These children are our children. Their future is our future."

'Ohana: family. "The essence of Hawai'i has always been that we come from far and wide, that we come from different backgrounds and different faiths, and different last names, and yet we come together as a single 'ohana because we believe in the fundamental commonality of people…Of all the rocks upon which we build our lives, we are reminded today that family is the most important."

Lōkahi: unity, harmony, agreement, creating unity. "It must be about what we can do together."

Mahalo: respect and thank you.

Ha'aha'a: humililty, modesty. "We look out for one another…we deal with each other with courtesy and respect. And most importantly, when you come from Hawai'i, you start understanding that what's on the surface, what people look like, doesn't determine who they are."

Pono: fair, just and good.

Ho'oponopono: working things out, resolving conflict, talking, listening, forgiving. "What people often note as my even temperament I think draws from Hawai'i… there just is a cultural bias toward courtesy and trying to work through problems in a way that makes everybody feel like they're being listened to."

"People ask me, they say, 'What do you still bring from Hawai'i?'…I try to explain to them something about the aloha spirit… And it's that spirit that I am absolutely convinced is what America is looking for right now."

Most of the quotes above come from the book, ***A President from Hawai'i*** *(Banana Patch Press, 2009).*

Hawaii: Cultures and Families in the 50th State

Hawaii became a state in 1959. I was fortunate as a child and young adult to visit every other state in the Union, including Alaska (the other distant state which joined the Union in 1959). Somehow, for me the islands of Hawaii remained distant, unapproachable, set in the middle of the Pacific Ocean. Finally, about twelve years ago, I visited Hawaii for the first time to attend a wedding. Since then I have visited the Big Island, Kauai, Maui, Oahu, Molokai, and Lanai.

Robbie watches Chance as the Sun sets

Interested in both archeology and culture, I'd like to share my reflections on the clash of cultures that I have seen on these trips. Hawaii is indeed a paradise, one with a tension based in cultural differences.

Consider a few questions:

What if the most important thing in your life is family? What if the most important thing in your life is nature? What *is* the most important thing in *your* life?

What happens when you meet and get to know someone whose most important thing is much different than yours?

We had just come back from Maui, Hawaii, and I thought about how different the feelings and most important things were to the people living there.

Those who have been there longest have generations of family going back hundreds of years. We saw large extended families gathered on beaches on weekends (and even other times) for joint meals and community time. Their ancestors had come to the island over thousands of miles of sea, following the stars and currents. They have established a culture and a connection to this warm and fertile land that is deep, lasting… and very spiritual.

Those who have relocated to Hawaii in recent years find themselves thousands of miles away from their families. They love the beauty and the warmth of the islands. They may have important goals of enjoying a lifestyle that includes material possessions and, perhaps, the means to get back to the families they left behind. Yes, it brings money and jobs to the island, and there is a 13% tourist tax in Hawaii that supports government services.

And many people from the mainland travel to enjoy the beauty and wonder of the islands for a very short time. They stay in places by the beach to swim and sit in the sun. Hawaiians use the beaches differently: big family BBQs, fishing and memorials to family members who have died.

What happens when these most important things meet in a place like Hawaii?

What happens when a large resort takes over a beach that was your family's sacred space and place to gather?

While the Hawaiian law says that *all beaches should have public access,* including trails to the beaches, there are often little or no parking spaces nearby and the access routes are difficult to find. Sometimes, the resorts make discouraging barriers for beach access.

We found that we enjoyed the beaches with easy access and with native people on them. However, we could also see why some beaches seemed set aside for specific purposes like kiteboarding or windsurfing. Some beaches were natural draws to surfers and snorkelers because of the way the ocean and shore come together.

When people from different cultural backgrounds meet, they have a choice to make: do we make assumptions about our right to impose our own way of knowing and being? Or, are we respectful and open? Certainly in Hawaii, there is much to gain from looking at the ways the Hawaiians have interacted with the natural world and the creatures in it.

As I left the islands I was reminded of my need to be open and caring with those I meet, particularly those whose culture is different than mine. I hope you will do the same in your interactions.

Cycle of Enlightenment

I have visited New York City a number of times in the last four years as my daughter is raising two of my grandchildren in Washington Heights, just north of Harlem. While I used to find the city dirty, and the people strange and distant, I have had a major transformation.

I now find the city wonderfully complex, the streets full of life, and the people amazingly friendly. For instance, not once did I have to carry my grandson-laden stroller up a long flight of stairs from the subway without someone, many ones actually, of all ages, races, genders, offering to lift up one end.

I know that the change has happened in my attitude—there has not been a sudden city-wide effort to make Jean feel comfortable.

Ah, how a few facts and a few days in a foreign country can make a difference.

You see, in New York City, I have always seen the people crunched in small apartments, using the stoops as meeting places and the street to wash or fix dilapidated cars as inherently *unhappy*. I had an elitist attitude towards the inhabitants of the Dominican neighborhood surrounding my daughter's family's apartment. How could anyone who lives in a concrete, noisy jungle with no individual transportation be happy? In particular, I pitied the poor worker who had only a bicycle to get to work in NYC or in my home state of Oregon.

However, I read an article in a recent *New Yorker Magazine* that explored the roots of happiness. Two research studies quoted continue to surprise me. For the first study, individuals who had either lost a leg or won the lottery were nearly back to their original biological set-point for happiness within a year of the event. Second, money directly correlated with happiness only under a very small minimum of $14,000 per year. Above that, happiness was more a matter of attitude than lack of basic survival resources. Only one factor under our individual control seems to consistently increase our happiness quotient: volunteering.

My other *aha* came from a short trip to Nicaragua. I visited at the invitation of a former student who was volunteering with JICA, the Japanese equivalent of the Peace Corps. Having lived in the country for two years and committed to live as the *Nicas*, she knew how to travel cheaply and she took me with her into her world. As the twentieth passenger added to a fifteen passenger van, I had a first-hand experience in appreciating any kind of gasoline-powered means of getting from one place to another. And once, while in such a van, we passed a family of four on one bicycle, a prized and treasured possession.

I realized that the people I saw on the crowded streets of New York or the rural roads of Nicaragua had many things that are the bedrock of happiness apart from money: family, friends, stimulation, community. How shallow my former perspective seemed.

Photos: Jean Moule in New York (left); and with children in Nicaragua (above).

Cultural Connections

My granddaughter, Ainsley in New York City, has a good friend named Octavia (see photo below). As I watched these two fourth graders practicing hurdles, I spoke to Octavia's mother, Asari Beale, about my column that helps bridge cultures. Asari began to tell me about Octavia's connections to another friend and how their worlds were both similar and different. Asari works with Reach Out and Read *of Greater New York, an organization that promotes children's literacy. She wrote the following story for this column.*

From Harlem to Chinatown

Octavia Beale squeezed her mother's hand as they climbed out of the subway station into the noisy streets of Chinatown. They had traveled there from their apartment way uptown in Harlem, to visit Octavia's friend Lauren. Though she had been there once before, she was still excited by the narrow winding streets cluttered with stores and restaurants and sidewalk vendors selling all kinds of fruits and vegetables. It was too exciting—being in a new part of town, and going to see her best friend—she yanked on her mom's arm and rushed forward. "Come on, hurry up! We're going to be late! Come on!!!"

"Slow down! We won't be late." Mrs. Beale knew this mood. When Octavia got excited about something, she could get as jumpy as a kitten in an aviary. Luckily, her mother knew just how to calm her down. She would distract Octavia with conversation.

"So," she began. "What is it that makes you and Lauren such good friends?"

"I don't know… Stuff. C'mon, mommy! The light is changing."

She pulled her mother across the street.

Mrs. Beale tried again, "Stuff like what?"

"Well… We both like building things and making up codes."

"That's true. What else?"

"We like to draw. We both like Harry Potter. Oh—and we both like to eat weird stuff, like rice balls and stuffed grape leaves."

"Those things don't seem so weird to me."

"Well, stuff other kids think is weird."

"I see."

Octavia was slowing down now, which was good.

Mrs. Beale's arm was already sore from all the pulling. She would need to keep the conversation going.

"I can think of something else you have in common," Mrs. Beale said.

"What?"

"You both live in ethnic neighborhoods."

Octavia thought about it a second. "Hey, that's true!"

Most of the people who live in Harlem are African or of African descent, and Harlem is known around the world as the center of Black American culture.

Octavia looked around. The busy storefronts and chatter of families in Chinatown reminded her of 125th Street in Harlem, where people came from around the city to shop, and where you could buy jewelry, books, and even African masks from sidewalk vendors.

Mrs. Beale went on. "And you both have grandparents from other countries."

"Yeah!" Octavia said. "Lauren's grandparents from her mom's side are Chinese…"

"And your *abuelo* and *abuela* are Panamanian. So you both have one side of your family that speaks a language other than English."

"I never thought of that before," Octavia said.

"Well, now you have. Hey, where are you going?"

Octavia looked confused. "To Lauren's apartment."

"But we're here."

Octavia looked up. "What? How did we get here so fast? We were talking so much, I didn't even realize…." She narrowed her eyes at her mother. "Mom, did you do that on purpose?"

Mrs. Beale shrugged. "What do you mean?" She hid her smile and held the door open. "Now, I know something you, Lauren and I all like: Lauren's grandmother's dumplings! I wonder if they'll have some for us."

"Let's find out!" Octavia shouted, and pulled her mother into the building.

What I Learned about Grandparenting in China

"I love that you are making the Chinese babies laugh! Laughter cuts across all language barriers!" said a friend while looking at this photo, and I thought how many things cross cultures naturally. For example, I find most babies and small children will laugh if I swing my hair. Then I stop, and there is a wonderful smile for a good photo; this is what happened at a temple in China we visited!

My husband, a.k.a. Pops or Popsie, enjoyed my connection with this child. He asked, "Did we enjoy our own children as much as we enjoy our grandchildren? And do other grandparents feel the same way?" He explained, the more transgenerational interactions he sees, the more he finds we, as grandparents, are not alone in feeling this way. Something happens between grandparents and their grandchildren that supplements what children are getting from their own parents. Whether grandparents are around because of financial difficulty, sickness, tradition or strong family ties, they have the ability to be positively involved in the development of their grandchildren, as well as receive love and emotional satisfaction from them in return.

Last July we had the opportunity to spend two weeks in China and were able to witness many examples of grandparents spending time with their grandchildren. In a country where most couples are only allowed to have one child, both parents and grandparents want the very best for their offspring. Many times families would encourage their children as young as eight or nine to approach us, ask how we were and welcome us to China. As children did this, in English, the parents and/or grandparents would be beaming with pride. During the day when both parents were working, the children, including infants, would be cared for by their grandparents. This is exactly what my photo of the grandbaby with a caring grandpa exhibits.

With our family, we have enhanced our ability to spend time with our far-flung grandchildren by having a *Cousins Camp* every summer. Each year there is a theme, and we often choose it a year ahead. Some themes we have had so far are Bunnies, Frogs, Dinosaurs, and this year, Birds. While we were in China I tried to get as many bird-themed items as possible. I found cloisonné birds, birds in jade, calligraphy birds, embroidered birds, painted birds, and a thoroughly annoying plastic parrot with a silly vocabulary.

Our program at our Cousins Camp this year included a live rooster, for that is both the shape and a symbol of China, as well as a play about birds interacting. The highlights though, were the contributions by two of the grandchildren who just happened to be studying China! Ainsley (6) and Bella (4) could both count in Chinese and tried to teach us grown ups. Bella sang an action song in Chinese, and we all joined in with the actions, though not the words.

Our memories of China and Chinese families were enhanced as we worked with our own grandchildren this summer. Our theme next year? Insects! And I already have some bugs embedded in plastic that I picked up in China.

Photos: Nana Jean in China (above); Jean holds another baby in Tanzania (right).

On European Customs

How do young children process culture when they travel and experience different languages, customs and clothing? I went with my family, including two of my grandchildren *(Photo: Jamie, 7, and Ainsley, 9)* for a week of travels in Italy. We skied in high mountains and walked among thousands in Venice.

Ainsley said, "In France and Spain, I could speak with the native people who live there. But Italians speak Italian, and I have not learned to speak Italian." She added, "It was a strange experience for me."

During our six days in Italy we did not see another family from the United States while we were skiing. We were very grateful that most of the people around us spoke English and were often eager to speak it with us. We found out that the children in the local school are first taught Italian, then Ladin, a regional language, and then English, beginning at age 7.

The differences in clothing had a strong impact on us. In Venice we watched a woman from a Middle Eastern culture go by in a gondola. Her hair and face were covered except for her eyes. It was strange for me and my grandchildren. They also noticed a difference when we went to the sauna in our *pension* in Corvara, Italy. "I cannot believe that the Europeans go in saunas naked!" Ainsley said. She was used to the custom in the United States of people entering saunas, hot tubs, and steam rooms in public places wearing their bathing suits. We talked at length about the differing custom. While I encouraged my grandchildren to wear bathing suits so they were comfortable, as is accepted in our culture in the United States, I also questioned their response to the more natural custom they saw in Italy. Is it *disgusting* and *gross*? No. It is just different. Respect for others' cultural differences starts with this simple understanding: differences do not mean *less than*, especially when traveling.

Another simple custom difference we found was how to get in and out of our rooms. In the United States, hotels usually give you a card key or a metal key for your room. In Europe, and many other places around the world, you almost always leave your room keys at the main desk when you are not in the hotel. It is usually attached to a large piece of leather or wood: too bulky to easily fit in your pocket. This custom allows the hotel to know when you are in your room or not. It also means you are less likely to take the key with you! It took us a few days to learn to automatically leave our key on the hook near the front desk.

In Italy, we noticed that there was more crowding to get into places and longer lines for ski lifts. Yet in the United Kingdom, we experienced very clear *queues,* or orderly lines for getting on buses and into other places. I believe some of these customs may vary quite a bit depending on regions within any country. At times, in the Dolomites of Italy, we found that if we were too polite and waited as we do in the U.S., it was a while before we got into a ski gondola or tram!

Then there was the process of getting service in places to eat. In Italy, I found I did not even know the simple way to get food in restaurants or *refugios,* on the mountains where we skied. Sometimes we ordered inside and the food was brought out. Other times we ordered at the tables. Because I do not know Italian, I had a difficult time finding out which to expect! Also, do you pay when you order? Or, do you pay when you are finished? Do you take your dishes to a collection station or leave them on your table? These simple understandings are *scripts*, often unspoken interactions that we come to know within our own culture or community, yet have difficulty understanding elsewhere. The children also noticed differences in the meals. Ainsley noted that "everybody eats much later than in the U.S." and "It's four-course meals!"

These differences have helped me pay more attention and be more adaptable. In our global world and our increasingly diverse classrooms, this is a skill we all need to practice.

What's in a Name?

This year, our family camping trip took place in Denali National Park in Alaska *(see photo)*. In addition to viewing moose, caribou, grizzly bears, Dall sheep, and the tallest peak in North America, we learned about the history of the region and its people.

For thousands of years, the Koyukon Athabascan people, who hunted and gathered beneath its summit, called it Denali, The High One. When Alaska was first settled by Russian explorers, they called it Bolshaya Gora, the Russian translation for *big mountain*. When the United States purchased Alaska from Russia in 1867 (derided at the time as *Seward's Folly*, after the decision by President Lincoln's Secretary of State), the American explorers and gold and silver prospectors continued to call it Denali.

But then, William Dickey, who was born in New Hampshire, educated at Princeton University in New Jersey, and resided in Seattle, came to Alaska in the 1896 gold rush. He didn't find much gold, but he wrote an account of his experiences that was published in a New York newspaper. He called the mountain McKinley, after the presidential candidate who became the country's 25th President. The name stuck.

It reportedly took two years for the news to get back to Alaska, and another two years for the people of the new Alaska Territory to register their disgust with the United States Congress. Congress still hasn't restored the original name, but Alaskans did in 1975, officially calling the mountain Denali on all state maps. The Denali National Park and Preserve was renamed in 1980, but the mountain continues to be called Mt. McKinley by the U.S. Board on Geographic Names.

Does it matter? What's in a name, anyway? For thousands of years, the local people called it by its description, the High One, and Alaskan Natives and other residents of Alaska still call it Denali. The mountain rising from the Alaskan Range is often shrouded in clouds, and only visible in part about a third of the time. We seldom see the great and high one in full view, and the history of the people who lived beneath the mountain for centuries is only partially understood.

Throughout the United States, many geographic features and places continue to be called by the names given by their Native residents. Think of the Mississippi or Ohio rivers; the 27 states with Native names, including Connecticut and Arkansas; and the

cities of Chicago and Manhattan. But what happened to the peoples who gave these features these names?

Who should name the land? And how should differences on naming be decided?

Many names that are offensive to the people who originally lived on the land have been changed, and there is a current effort to change team and mascot names that have negative impacts on Native Americans.

There is considerable controversy over many team names and mascots because various groups, including some representing indigenous peoples, view them as disrespectful, racist, and offensive. The National Congress of American Indians, the largest organization representing enrolled tribal citizens in the United States, issued a resolution opposing continued usage of Native American team names, mascots, and logos by non-Native teams. Numerous educational, academic, civil rights, athletic, and religious organizations have done the same. At the same time many teams and fans support the continued use of these names as a long-standing tradition, and cite public opinion polls indicating the names are not offensive to a majority, including Native Americans. The Internet contains many more details about this issue under "Native American mascot controversy." When naming teams and physical features of the land, names and their cultural contexts *do* matter!

A nursery rhyme says, "Sticks and stones may break my bones, but words can never hurt me." This may be true in a physical sense, but words and language can cause deep and lasting emotional pain. Please think about the words you use and the names you call others. Mountains don't have feelings, but people do.

Written by Jean and her daughter, Mary Ellen Moule.
P.S. In Aug. 2015, the U.S. Dept. of the Interior announced that it was officially renaming Mt. McKinley as Denali.

Understanding Cultures

Culture is a difficult concept. It is so basic to human societies and so intertwined with our natures that its workings are seldom acknowledged or thought about. It is so all-encompassing, like water to a fish, that it remains largely preconscious and is obvious only when it is gone or has been seriously disturbed. Anthropological definitions point to certain aspects. Culture is composed of traditional ideas and related values; it is learned, shared, and transmitted from one generation to the next; and it organizes and helps interpret life. The iceberg diagram illustrates the difference between surface and deep culture. Like an iceberg, nine-tenths of culture is below the surface. As you see on the iceberg, food, dress, music, visual arts, drama, crafts, dance, literature, language, celebrations and games are the surface forms of culture.

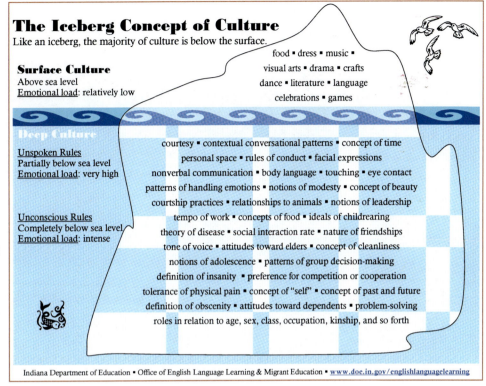

The Iceberg Concept of Culture
Like an iceberg, the majority of culture is below the surface.

Surface Culture
Above sea level
Emotional load: relatively low
- food • dress • music • visual arts • drama • crafts • dance • literature • language • celebrations • games

Deep Culture

Unspoken Rules
Partially below sea level
Emotional load: very high

Unconscious Rules
Completely below sea level
Emotional load: intense

- courtesy • contextual conversational patterns • concept of time
- personal space • rules of conduct • facial expressions
- nonverbal communication • body language • touching • eye contact
- patterns of handling emotions • notions of modesty • concept of beauty
- courtship practices • relationships to animals • notions of leadership
- tempo of work • concepts of food • ideals of childrearing
- theory of disease • social interaction rate • nature of friendships
- tone of voice • attitudes toward elders • concept of cleanliness
- notions of adolescence • patterns of group decision-making
- definition of insanity • preference for competition or cooperation
- tolerance of physical pain • concept of "self" • concept of past and future
- definition of obscenity • attitudes toward dependents • problem-solving
- roles in relation to age, sex, class, occupation, kinship, and so forth

Indiana Department of Education • Office of English Language Learning & Migrant Education • www.doe.in.gov/englishlanguagelearning

A specific example of how surface and deep culture interact is given by my colleague, Valerie Pang. A surface artifact in the Japanese culture is origami; we will use the paper-folding of a crane, a classroom activity I have witnessed. The customs, practices, and interactional patterns are observable:

1. Child watches another child or adult fold paper.

2. Child folds paper one section at a time, modeling the "teacher."

3. Teacher waits patiently and shows folds several times if needed.

4. Child and teacher treat each other with respect.

Yet, below the surface, there is deep culture. There are shared values, beliefs, norms, and expectations:

1. Develops a sense of patience

2. Reinforces a sense of community

3. Teaches respect for the teacher or for someone with skill

4. Cranes represent good luck and long life in Japanese culture

5. Reflects value of simplicity and beauty

People grow emotionally attached to their cultural specifics and give up or change them only with great difficulty and discomfort. A challenge to one's culture is experienced as a personal threat, for ego gets invested in the portrayal of how things should be. When the world no longer operates as it *should*, people feel cut adrift from familiar moorings, no longer sure where they stand or who they are.

Culture provides content: identity, beliefs, values, and behavior. It is learned as part of the natural process of growing up in a family and community and from participating in societal institutions. From this perspective, it is easy to understand why the imposition of one group's culture upon members of another cultural group may be experienced so negatively. This often occurs in bicultural families, where the European culture is the standard against which Children of Color —who may come to view their world through different eyes—are measured.

Even though many individuals experience a world more defined by skin color than by culture, we may turn to cultural differences as a useful and less controversial yardstick than race.

Material excerpted from *Cultural Competence: A Primer for Educators* by Jean Moule

A Letter from My Colleague and Artist Friend

Dear Jean,

Where do I start to describe the influences we have had on each other as close friends and colleagues? My first recollection of meeting you was when you interviewed as a doctoral student in our teacher education program with your leg in a cast. Little did I know at that time what a role model you would be to me as my first true African American friend and colleague. Not only have you inspired me, but I find you awe-inspiring! As somewhat of an introvert, I see you "work the crowds" at conferences and am always envious as to how you can just walk up to someone and find a commonality that often extends beyond the conference walls. Walking into a room full of strangers is one of my greatest fears and you seem to thrive on it. One day, not too long ago, I told you how I saw you as being so courageous and outgoing-and how I wanted to be like you. Then, you told me how you had to work at it and held many of the same fears as myself. I was truly surprised.

I think of so many of our journeys over the past 20 years and how you have inspired me. One of our closest times was when we worked in the "Immersion" program which brought us together with a group of students for a three-week experience in a Portland inner-city elementary school. We spent almost every waking hour with each other and you opened my eyes by sharing your perspectives with me. It was such a powerful experience for me, and we came together afterwards writing up our research on the project—sharing the richness of our perspectives and how our cultural lenses shaped what we saw and didn't see. I always learn so much from you and you allow me to question and share my naivety with you. "Well, Karen, did you ever think about it this way?" I can honestly say you have helped shape the very core of who I am. I do not say that lightly.

Breaks during our writing led us to geocaching, climbing mountains, and lots of laughter as well as tears —plus a little wine. I will never forget our week together in Cabo San Lucas. We found every geocache there. You were an inspiration to me when you climbed a very scary rocky hill, determined to find that cache. But then, someone had to watch our things, right?? We have camped, boated, hunted for chanterelles, and shared our wildest dreams. When you went sky-diving for your 50th birthday—Yikes!!! Talk about a role model.

When my husband was dying of cancer, you were there helping me cope. Along with my other colleagues, you shared some of the burden of my workload so I could be with him. Now, as your husband Robbie has his own struggles with cancer, I have been able to talk openly with you and validate so many of your own feelings. Strange how situations like this take on a different meaning when we can talk to someone who has already walked the path with us. There is an intimacy that's hard to describe. Although reliving memories is sometimes difficult (as you have so graciously helped me understand in so many ways), reliving with you somehow makes the memories more meaningful.

One of the most amazing things that has brought us together recently is our artwork. I had no idea what an artist you were, and we have taken great pleasure in sharing our work with each other. I still have fond memories of our painting together. Watching you negotiate a table in Cabo so we could paint outside just made me shake my head and giggle. "That's my Jean!" Yes, truly an inspiring role model.

Well, Jean, I could go on and on, but I think I'll stop here. I know we have many more adventures together and the complexities of this amazing friendship I have with you will continue to inspire me and help me grow.

Thank you!

karen

Photo: Jean & Karen Higgins on the beach, Cabo San Lucas, Mexico.

Inspiring Role Models

In the light of daring, caring, risking, dreaming and expecting more than what seems possible, practical or wise at first, role models may help you and your grandchildren aim high.

Bessie Coleman: African American Aviatrix

Who was one of the first Americans to hold an international pilot license?

As a challenge, I decided that I wanted to learn to fly a small airplane. My flight instructor knew I needed to learn about other Black women who had flown. First, he connected me to a Black female student pilot. Then he introduced me to the legendary Bessie Coleman.

Bessie was born in Texas in 1892 as one of 13 children of a couple who worked in the cotton fields. She was good at math, loved books, and walked eight miles round trip to attend a one-room school for Blacks. She went to Oklahoma where she studied for one term at a university, but had to leave due to lack of money.

In 1915, at age 23, Bessie moved to Chicago. She lived with her brothers and worked as a fingernail manicurist in the city. In Chicago, she heard and read stories of World War I soldiers and pilots as they returned from Europe. She and her brother, a soldier, talked.

"Those French women do something no Colored girl has done," her brother teased. "They fly."

Taking that as a challenge, Bessie decided to become a pilot. Due to both race and gender discrimination, she gave up trying to enter a flight school in the United States and began her study of French. She learned the language well enough to grasp the principles of flight and the technical aeronautic terms in that language. Then she went to France to learn to fly.

She completed a ten-month course in just seven months to receive her pilot's license. She returned to the U. S. to fly. She wanted to start flight schools for African Americans. She earned her living barnstorming and performing aerial tricks, specializing in stunt flying and parachuting.

Bessie's high-flying skills wowed audiences of thousands. She was well known all over the United States, making big headlines whenever she flew in air shows.

During a rehearsal for an air show in 1926, she leaned out of an airplane flown by her mechanic to check her planned parachute-landing site. The plane began an unexpected tailspin towards the ground.

Bessie, who was unbelted at the time, was thrown out of the plane and fell 1,500 feet to her death.

Afterwards others took up her cause to begin flight schools that allowed Blacks' entry. Some of those inspired by her daring learned to fly in these schools and were early enrollees in the World War II Black Tuskegee Airmen Division. I found out that my grandson's great-grandfather was a flight instructor for those airmen!

Bessie's legacy continued on through the years. In 1929, the aviation school she worked to establish was founded in Los Angeles. Roads, highways and flying clubs for women were named after her. In 1995, the U.S. Postal Service issued a Bessie Coleman stamp. And every year on Memorial Day, the Tuskegee Airmen fly over Brave Bessie's grave and drop flowers in her honor.

Bessie Coleman once said, "Do you know that you have never lived until you have flown?" While few fly in small airplanes, many people have been able to fly in large jets. My children have all flown commercially, as have my grandchildren. One grandchild, Chance, the great grandson of Tuskegee Airman instructor, James A. Hill, leads the rest: before he was five years old he had flown on 120 flight segments.

For leading the way, I give my thanks to Elizabeth "Bessie" Coleman, one of the first American aviators to hold a license to fly anywhere in the world, the first female pilot of African descent, and a pioneer in aviation education for all people.

Nana Jean with grandson Chance.

Jean Faces A Challenge

"*75765, is there an instructor on board?*" My erratic taxiing had been noted by the control tower.

The basics of flying seemed so difficult. Maybe it was a good thing that the threatening weather kept my instructor and me on the ground in our plane. I stared through the raindrops on the aircraft windshield. Would I ever learn to fly?

I have seen my grandchildren and my students begin a difficult task, become frustrated and put the material or task down with a sigh, lacking the will to continue. I have learned how to help them move past the barriers and try again. Could I do that for myself?

Rarely in my adult life have I faced tasks I found challenging beyond learning a new skill on the computer or how to work a new appliance or gadget. And rarely do these tasks have high emotional impact or the kinds of pressure one may experience when the task is complex, cognitively difficult and watched over intently by a teacher.

Perhaps I needed a reminder of such experiences. Five years ago in *Ask Nana Jean*, I wrote about my climb up Mount Kilimanjaro in Tanzania and concluded with my desire to reach more heights. Climb another mountain? Learn to fly? And that is how I found myself behind the controls of an airplane, in the pilot's seat with the instructor on the controls on my right. Could I reach high places in a plane?

This was my third lesson; this time with a substitute instructor. The checklist with 120 items and a cockpit with a lot more dials than a car seemed bewildering. Afterwards, as I paid for my half hour on the ground my head filled over and over with "Why am I doing this?" I reminded myself why I wanted to learn to fly:

- Because I like heights
- Because I want additional perspectives
- Because I need exhilaration and a new challenge

I drove home feeling dejected, the rain and gray clouds matching my mood. I knew that at some point I would have to find the reserves to try again. I tried to encourage myself by thinking about other challenging things I have accomplished:

- Learning to drive a car
- Handling an excavator
- Learning to ski or pull a sled while on ski patrol
- Learning to teach!

I made a list of resolutions and requests that I believed would help me continue on:

- Get a copy of the preflight checklist and go over it at home
- Get a life-sized poster of the cockpit and practice touching the right switches
- Ask my instructor to taxi next time to at least get us off the ground

And finally, I remembered the pleasure I receive when my own students begin to grasp a concept that is hard for them. So my final reason for continuing with my lessons? My instructors may feel blessed when their challenging and challenged student finally makes progress. They, too, will have a student whose success they will remember fondly…when she finally learns to fly solo.

Ten days later, my journal entry read:

I flew today. My instructor watched as I turned the plane over our house, circled the small town of Lyons where we used to live, and flew over the road I take to work. Up and down. Level flight, smooth turns and a deep satisfaction. Now, I need to learn to take off and land!

What a contrast to just a few days ago when I almost put down my pilot log-book for good.

My words for myself and others, "When the journey gets tough, be strong and continue on. No matter how long it takes."

Rosa Parks: One Person Makes a Difference

Rosa Parks has become a symbol of the Civil Rights Movement and an international icon. Yet, more importantly for everyone, she is an image of one lone person taking a stance that made a very big difference. She was sitting in a part of the bus that allowed *Colored* (African American) people unless it was needed for a White rider. When she was asked to move back to make room for a White passenger she would not. Rosa was 42 years old at the time and she was no more tired than anyone would be after a long day of work. She said, *"The only tired I was, was tired of giving in."*

Recently I was asked to talk about Rosa Parks to observe her birthday, February 4.

I was excited reading about her on Wikipedia, mostly because I saw a few parallels in my own life. We both saw discrimination from a young age. Rosa Parks said, *"As far back as I remember, I could never think in terms of accepting physical abuse without some form of retaliation if possible."*

Rosa Parks and I were both adults during the Civil Rights Movement. She was arrested in Montgomery, Alabama, and I during the Free Speech Movement at the University of California at Berkeley. I sat on the floor of the main administration building to protest an attempt to keep people from speaking their beliefs on our public campus. There were hundreds and hundreds of us. Our numbers made this work. Yet Rosa Parks protested and was arrested alone.

Rosa said, *"I did not want to be mistreated, I did not want to be deprived of a seat that I had paid for. It was just time… there was opportunity for me to take a stand to express the way I felt about being treated in that manner. I had not planned to get arrested. I had plenty to do without having to end up in jail. But when I had to face that decision, I didn't hesitate to do so because I felt that we had endured that too long. The more we gave in, the more we complied with that kind of treatment, the more oppressive it became."*

I share a seat with the memorial statue of Rosa Parks at the entrance to the Lane Transit District's Downtown Eugene Bus Station.

Rosa was not the first person to be arrested for sitting in a seat considered wrong by the bus company, the police, and most of the community. However, her arrest galvanized others to act. The next day began a long bus boycott in the city of Montgomery, Alabama.

The day of her trial a handbill read, *"We are…asking every Negro to stay off the buses Monday in protest of the arrest and trial…You can afford to stay out of school for one day. If you work, take a cab, or walk. But please, children and grown-ups, don't ride the bus at all on Monday. Please stay off the buses. Monday."* And they did. Some people walked 20 miles at first. The boycott lasted for 381 days, until victory was at hand.

Park's legacy spread far and wide. Mine extends just a few ripples but I know that I am willing to stand up for what I believe. I am willing to be arrested. I am willing to try to make a difference when I see people being treated unfairly. I have walked a picket by myself. I have been the only person at a meeting willing to state a viewpoint that was different than those around me.

I look to people like Rosa Parks as examples of what one person may accomplish. When I got arrested over 50 years ago I was doing what I believed was the right thing to do. It reminds me even today to be firm and sometimes work against the grain.

One of my favorite quotes (from Albert Einstein) is *"The one who follows the crowd will usually get no further than the crowd. The one who walks alone is likely to find himself in places no one has ever been,"* like being arrested for sitting in a bus.

In an issue of *Skipping Stones*, I discussed a simple way one may speak out against stereotypes, read this column on the next page.

My TV interview on Rosa Parks and Standing Up is at: http://youtu.be/_O2ctn_MC80

—*Jean Moule, PhD, author, artist, activist, and FSM arrestee.*

On Speaking Up

"Stereotype" means to believe, incorrectly, that all people or things with a particular characteristic are the same.

What do you do when you hear someone say something about a group or an individual that could be hurtful? Have you heard someone speak in a manner that made you uncomfortable and you wished you had a response? Martin Luther King, Jr. said, "In the end we will remember not the words of our enemies, but the silence of our friends." Displaying an attitude that one way, or group, is better than another, often leads to deep hurt and physical violence.

Years ago a student in one of my classes gave me an article, *Addressing Prejudiced Statements: A Four Step Method that Works!* by Beatrice Fennimore.

To demonstrate this in my classes and workshops, I open the floor for anyone to give me a statement, either mild or awful, and I come up with a response on the spot. Sometimes my words are halting and limited.

Many people do not feel comfortable about confronting prejudiced statements. Perhaps, they feel that the speaker will get angry or stop liking them, or that they will be mean to them, too. They might feel like they can't make a difference. Letting statements go unchallenged not only misses a chance to confront what could be biased, but silence can also be taken as agreement. If you practice confronting negative statements, you'll become more comfortable when you find yourself in such situations. The four-step process allows people to gently correct a prejudiced statement without creating a climate of rejection or bad feelings.

I suggest we must respond; better imperfect words than silence. By speaking up, we can work to support the dignity and equality of people, especially our friends, both inside and outside of schools.

Four-Step Response to Prejudiced Statements:

1. Pull the prejudice out of the comment and restate it in a calm and objective way.
2. State personal beliefs in a clear and assertive manner.
3. Make a positive statement about the specific subjects of the prejudice.
4. Gently turn the subject to a new direction.

My son teaches middle school, and I asked him to give me some examples of prejudicial comments he has heard from students. Below are three examples of prejudiced statements and possible four-step responses:

"How come you don't watch TV? Is your family poor?"

- You believe that watching TV is something that everyone would enjoy, if they could. *(Step 1)*
- I know many people who prefer other ways to spend time than watching TV. *(Step 2)*
- Young people who watch less TV have more time for reading, sports, and hanging out with friends. *(Step 3)*
- What books are you reading now? *(Step 4)*

"Ayan is from Somalia; we can catch Ebola from him."

- Some children think that everyone from Africa carries Ebola. *(Step 1)*
- I've been following this tragic story, so I know that Ebola is a problem in West Africa, and has not spread to East, North, or Southern Africa. *(Step 2)*
- Somalia is far away from West Africa, where Ebola is. Many Somali refugees came here to escape civil war that was difficult for them in East Africa. *(Step 3)*
- We can all work to stay healthy and keep disease from spreading by washing our hands well and often. *(Step 4)*

"How can you eat food that does not have meat in it, just vegetables. It's not healthy."

- I know that many who eat meals that have meat in them cannot understand why someone may choose meals with beans, grains, fruits, nuts, vegetables. *(Step 1)*
- I have studied the food pyramid and I know that balanced meals do not have to include meat. *(Step 2)*
- My sister is a vegetarian. She finds it easy to plan healthy meals. My niece is vegan and feels it's better for health (and nature) not to eat animal products. *(Step 3)*
- Next time there's a potluck, try some vegetarian dishes. What are your favorite pizza toppings? *(Step 4)*

Practicing responses to prejudicial statements with someone you trust makes it easier to speak up in a situation where silence may indicate that you agree with a statement. Let one person make a prejudiced statement. The other person thinks up and shares their four-step response without being interrupted. In real situations, if you are bold and speak up clearly and gently, you may make a difference in that moment. Speak up, because, in the struggle for justice, we all need to be friends.

About Role Models like Yourself

First Lady Michelle Obama was the commencement speaker at Oregon State University on June 17, 2012. I wrote this letter to her.

Dear Michelle,

As far as I know, you are the second woman of African descent to speak at an Oregon State University commencement. I was the speaker for the 2003 graduate ceremony. At that time the graduations were separated: the undergraduates had a "guest" speaker and the graduate students had a faculty member. I was both honored and humbled to be chosen to give a 12-minute address that June day to the Masters and Doctoral candidates.

I plan to be in the audience on the 17th as a faculty representative and I look forward to it all: the excitement, the security, and the incredible opportunity to listen to a female speaker who reflects my hue. This is simply beyond my wildest expectations. As an activist and one who has been part of the struggle, your presence speaks of much progress.

Thank you for coming. I do hope the day goes very well for you.

I am emeritus now in the College of Education. This event will be the last time I will wear my academic regalia, passing it on to my lawyer daughter who will wear it in her duties as a college trustee at Voorhees College.

I thought you might like to read the speech I gave.

The best to you, First Lady Michelle.

Professor Jean Moule

I received a gracious form letter reply from the White House. While I doubt the First Lady ever read my speech, I have a warmer spot in my heart for her speech because I tried to share mine. I was seated in the first row, but I could see her much better on the large screens. I was struck by her humility and enthusiasm. Her speech addressed neither the presidential politics nor race relations.

Of the many things she shared with the graduates and their families and friends, one theme struck home for me: What is a measure of success? First of all, she said, "The true measure of your success is… not how well you do when you're healthy, and happy and everything is going according to plan. But what you do when life knocks you to the ground and all your plans go right out the window. In those darkest moments, you have a choice: Do you dwell on everything you've lost? Or do you focus on what you still have, and find a way to move forward with passion, and determination, and joy?"

Mrs. Obama further defined the importance of passion over money for a career choice. She then told us the story of her and her brother's struggles to succeed in school, through college and in their early careers (her brother was a coach at OSU). "We soon had all the traditional markers of success—the fat paycheck, the fancy office, the impressive line on our resumes. But the truth is, neither of us was all that fulfilled. I didn't want to be up in some tall office building writing legal memos; I wanted to be down on the ground, helping the folks I grew up with. I was living the dream—but it wasn't my dream."

By the world's and by money's standards, they were both highly successful. Yet their jobs in finance and law were not inspiring. Each choose to take less money for more personal satisfaction. They redefined success for themselves. And in that choice rose spectacularly in their new fields of coaching and service.

The most emotional moment for me came when the graduating students, who were also in one of the campus military officer training units, were commissioned. Before the First Lady, they took an oath of office with their hands over their hearts. As they finished, two military jets flew over. It was a thrilling sight!

Mrs. Obama left after the degrees were conferred and while graduates were lining up to receive their diplomas. It was a last event for me as a faculty member in my gown. It was a first for me to see the wife of the highest official in the land surrounded by pomp, circumstance and high security, walking in her brown skin and regal bearing to give inspiration and encouragement to us all.

Let's Make a Difference in Our World

As a guide on the side, I ask my students to select a guiding quote: something that means a lot to them, something they read in a book, something they heard from a famous person or even a relative. I often borrow these quotes from my students and put them where they can help me! The one by my phone reminds me, *"The first step to wisdom is silence; the second is listening."* The quote on my computer gets me through writer's block: *"I can do all things through Him who strengthens me."* And the quote over my desk quiets my frustrations with: *"You may not be able to change the world, but at least you can embarrass the guilty."*

Our quote for now is, *"A genius is someone who aims for something that no one else can see…and hits it."* I would like you to find a use for this quote. Take a moment to put in another word for *genius* if you like. You could insert *innovator* or *risk-taker* or "one who makes a difference" or "going-to-get-this-done hard worker" if you wish.

Often, I close my eyes and think about whether or not to aim for something very difficult or out of reach. Sometimes it works out, sometimes not. When it does, I am encouraged to aim a bit higher and a little farther.

I recall a time that I aimed high, reaching for a mark that my teacher could not see. I disliked the way history was taught with monocultural perspectives, and I had to repeat a U.S. History class in summer school. I put my heart into it this time and wrote a stirring, creative beginning to my paper on the Oregon Trail. My teacher did not believe me, an African American student, when I told her I wrote it myself. Discouraged by her low expectations of minority students, I did not bother finishing the research paper and received another low grade. Her harshness and her assumptions hampered my interest in writing as well as in history.

Much later, as a classroom teacher, I found Oregon history peculiarly intriguing: Oregon hosted on its soil a moment of inclusion when York, a Black man who was Clark's slave, and Sacajawea, a Native woman, voted along with the rest of the Lewis & Clark Expedition for the location of its winter camp. Yet, Oregon's history is marred by racist laws. One law assessed blacks, Chinese and Hawaiians an annual $5 tax for the privilege of living in Oregon. This legacy of exclusion is seen today in the absence of people of color in many Oregon communities.

Reaching higher can be as simple as not telling or reacting to racist jokes. A quote from one of my students: *"I will never tell a racist joke, so I'm not racist, but… I have laughed at other people's racist jokes,"* and later in the course, *"It will never again be okay to laugh at a racist joke or even to keep silent when one is being told."* These students are beginning to understand their own roles in the subtle, often-hidden racism that surrounds us all. Every term, my students report to me that when they take the time to open their eyes, they notice that while shopping, driving or meeting, people of color are treated differently. One said, *"Race shouldn't matter, but in this country, it still does—to everybody."*

On a more complex level, let's consider my own case. I am one of very few African American faculty members at Oregon State University. What is it like to be this brown face in a sea of whiteness?

"It is as if we are all on a river that flows quietly and gently along. Most of my friends, students, and colleagues float on this river in a strong, sturdy boat of their majority status—a boat I cannot get into because I am not White. The river, our societal mainstream, is accepted and hardly noticed. I manage to swim or float alongside the boat as I am learning how to navigate this mainstream. Every once in a while someone in the boat notices my struggle and tosses out an inner tube or briefly holds my hand. And then sometimes, someone reaches out and pushes my head under with, 'Just get over this race thing, Jean.' I sputter, resurface and continue on. In the long run, I figure it makes sense to construct a raft for myself. So while I talk to those in the boat and we run difficult rapids together, at the same time I must lash together whatever supportive materials I can find. The response? 'Hey, how come Jean gets a raft?' If I say, 'Because I can't get in the boat with you and I'm getting tired of staying afloat without more support.' Some of them say, 'What boat?'"

We all struggle with the complex issues raised by this metaphor, whether it applies to race or other areas of difference. The challenge for those in the water and for those in the boat is to reach out for each other on our common journey while aiming to make a difference in the very river that carries us all along.

May you have many wonderful experiences as you work to make a difference in your world.

A longer version of this 2003 commencement address to Oregon State University graduates appears in Jean's book, **Cultural Competence** *(Cengage Learning).*

Continuing On

As I continue to explore and explain, I hope to help parents, grandparents, and educators on their journeys. May the insights from this book help those who choose to venture into this challenge and those whom they welcome into the world as offspring or grandchildren.

The travelers stopped to rest. They looked back the way they had come. The path seemed longer and more difficult than they had remembered. Their talk as they walked must have helped to smooth the way. Now that they had the vantage point of the ridge, they saw that what they perceived as a summit had been the beginning of the foothills. They continued on…

I would like to thank my family and friends for guidance, course corrections, and calling my attention to the sights, if not the misspellings. My children, Mary, Michael and Matt and their partners, encouraged access to and stories about their children. My friends, especially Bonnie, Karen, Patty, Paul, and Shelaswau, enhanced this work specifically and generously. Arun, there would be no columns without your bimonthly prompting, and your wonderful interns. And to my partner for 50 years, Rob, continue on and strong.

Gratitude expands outward to those I have forgotten and those I will encounter.

About the Author: Jean Moule was born in South Carolina and raised in New York City and Los Angeles. She earned her bachelor's from the University of California at Berkeley, where she studied art, psychology, and education, and was arrested in the Free Speech Movement. She earned her master's from the University of Oregon and doctorate from Oregon State University. Her words of inspiration come from her education, experiences, and her talks with three children, six grandchildren, and many friends. She hopes that her work will help the nation's children, including her grandchildren, to live in culturally competent families and communities. Visit Jean at www.jeanmoule.com.

Made in the USA
Middletown, DE
22 May 2017